The Writing Party

Ken Waldman

The Writing Party

Ken Waldman

Copyright 2020 © Ken Waldman
All rights reserved
ISBN: 978-0-9994784-8-6
Library of Congress
Control Number: 2020931904

Book Design: Jerry Hagins

Mezcalita Press, LLC
Wimberley, Texas
www.mezpress.com

MEZCALITA PRESS

This book is for all writers, writing teachers, and anyone curious how a particular writer and writing teacher has made a life doing this work. Thanks, too, to Jeff Talmadge, who read an earlier draft and helped this to be.

No part of this book may be performed, recorded, or otherwise transmitted without the written consent of the author and the permission of the publisher. However portions of the poems may be cited for book reviews without obtaining such consent. Contact Mezcalita Press, LLC or go to kenwaldman.com for more information.

2 3 4 5 6 7 8 9 10

Ken Waldman combines Appalachian-style string-band music, original poetry, and mostly Alaska-set storytelling for a performance uniquely his. Touring full-time since 1995, he's appeared at some of North America's leading concert series, performing arts centers, festivals, colleges, and clubs. He has 9 CDs (including 2 for children), 14 books (11 full-length poetry collections, a memoir, a kids' book, this hybrid volume), and a knack for putting together shows specific to place. His mix of words and music has had him compared to everyone from John Hartford to Ken Burns to Walt Whitman. He's been featured at the Kennedy Center Millennium Stage, The Dodge Poetry Festival, the Woodford Folk Festival (Queensland, Australia), and numerous other venues. A former college professor with an MFA from University of Alaska Fairbanks, he's led hundreds of writing workshops from Alaska to Maine. kenwaldman.com and trumpsonnets.com

Mezcalita Press, LLC was founded by touring musician and former Poet Laureate of Oklahoma, Nathan Brown, and his wife, Ashley Brown, a writer, editor, and teacher. Their mission is to publish necessary books by those writers who are also touring musicians. mezpress.com

Contents

Introduction 1
1: Icebreaker 8
2: Creating Character: Names From A-Z 20
3: The Dictionary Game 29
4: Occasionally Acrostic, and Other Wordplay 43
5: Repetition, Not Rhyme: The Sounds of the Fiddle 52
6: The Poetry Olympics (Yes, Sometimes Poems
   Definitely Rhyme) 59
7: Postcards, Anyone? 66
8: The Object Is 73
9: Talk, Talk, Talk 82
10: Read, Read, Read 87
11: Speaking of Voices 92
12: Poetry as Headlines (And Poetry as News) 97
13: Three Short Lessons, Compliments of Professor B 103
14: Writer as Scavenger, Poet as Sculptor 106
15: One Minute (Life or Death) 110
16: Places, Imaginary and Not 115
17: Holiday and Family 126
18: Failed Novelist (Self-Sabotage and Other Sports) 137
19: Indignities 142
20: 21 Sentences (A Narrative Guide) 152
21: Table For One (Under House Arrest) 155
22: A Party of Resources (Two Books, Six Websites,
   Thirty-Four Poems) 162
23: A Party of Sonnets (Thirty-Four Poems
   About Writers) 210
24: How I Make a Living in Poetry (A Review
   and Summary) 244
25: Three Essays 252
26: A Manifesto 279
27: Endings 283

Acknowledgments:
Grateful acknowledgment is made to the editors of the following books, anthologies, and journals in which some of these pieces, or versions of these pieces, first appeared, or will appear:

Books
Nome Poems: "Nine Pieces of Paper" "Class Party, Nome"
To Live on This Earth: "After Hearing John Haines Read" "Old-Time Fiddle Lesson" "Fairbanks Cabin" "William Stafford Atop Mt. Ripinski"
The Secret Visitor's Guide: "Bill Stafford" "15,000 Feet, Denali" "John Haines, Fairbanks, June 2004"
And Shadow Remained: "Satan Found!"

Anthologies
A Ritual to Read Together: Poems in Conversation with William Stafford: "Villanelle for William Stafford"
Obsession: Sestinas in the 21st Century: "The Substitute Teaches the Sestina"

Journals
Bard: "Author at Nine"
Barnabe Mountain Review: "William Stafford Atop Mt. Ripinski"
Blue Unicorn: "Native Writer"
Chariton Review: "Bill Stafford"
Controlled Burn: "Roethke House, After Hours"
Embers: "Second Best Friends"
Florida Reading Quarterly: "She Asked Where Poems Come From" "Heigh-Ho Silver, Away"
High Plains Literary Review: "Fairbanks Cabin"
Ice-Floe: "After Hearing John Haines Read"
Interim: "Fire Song"
Kansas Quarterly/Arkansas Review: "Walt Whitman's Visit"
KYSO: "Writer as Scavenger, Poet as Sculptor"
Lilliput Review: "Poems"
The MacGuffin: "A Short Story Formula" "Black Hair, Purple Lips"
New Delta Review: "Writing Class, The Correctional Center"
Onionhead: "The Lode"
Plainsongs: "Another Generation"
Poetry Flash: "Crowdfunding for Poets (and Other Contrarians)"
Poets & Writers: "How I Make a Living in Poetry"
Pudding: "Class Party, Nome" "Writing Lesson" "A History of Reading"
Red Savina Review: "Upon Rereading Richard Hugo" "Hemingway Spots Faulkner in a Bar"
Quarterly West: "Frank Leopold, Jr."
Rag Mag: "Father and Son"
San Diego Poetry Annual: "Frost Place"
Terrain.org: "Bill Stafford, 100" "Sestina for William Stafford"
Toad Suck Review: "Going Pubic"
Uncle: "The Substitute Teaches the Sestina"
Wordwrights: "The Day After Bukowski Died" "Emeritus"
Yemassee: "To the Author"

Introduction

The romanticized image of a writer holed-up alone—and I'm doing precisely that as I type these words—ignores the feedback from early readers, the essential support of family and friends, the growing use of writing coaches, the contributions of agents, editors, and publishers.

It also ignores the proliferation of writing workshops, whether formal or informal, in academic, conference, or community settings.

The image also ignores a conundrum. These days writers do what they've always done. These days writers do what they've never before done.

Now over sixty years old, I've been at this long enough to have done, at least in passing, plenty of the things that contemporary writers and writing teachers do. A late bloomer, I began a three-year residential MFA program just as I was turning thirty. After graduating, I continued to write, spending a year juggling part-time jobs, then a year as a visiting assistant professor, then two years as a tenure-track assistant professor.

Since then, for more than twenty years I've been a freelance writer, teacher, musician, and performer. As a writer, I've had over 400 poems and stories in literary journals, and have had eleven poetry collections and a memoir published by long-established independent presses. My self-published children's book, written to pair with my second children's CD, was quickly picked up for distribution by University of Alaska Press.

I've been a visitor at over a hundred colleges and universities, sometimes just to share my work publicly, other times to also go into classrooms, where occasionally the students have been assigned one of my books. I've attended many other kinds of workshops, both as participant and instructor, and have been a visiting artist at over two hundred schools in more than thirty states, sometimes working with high school students who are doing MFA-level work, and sometimes working with kindergartners who are just learning to read and write.

As a musician, I'm a fiddler who has recorded nine CDs that combine old-time Appalachian-style string-band music with original poetry. As a performer, I combine the music, the poetry, and Alaska-set storytelling, and appear in a wide variety of venues, from intimate coffeehouses to 1,500-seat theaters where I might bring a troupe of fellow musicians.

Increasingly, I've learned how to better describe myself and my work.

I sometimes say I'm of the William Stafford school, which has meant I've aimed to be inclusive rather than exclusive as a writer, as a teacher, and as a human. When asked my favorite writer, I'll often answer Stafford, and since in many of the places I go he's an unfamiliar name, I'll then quickly describe him.

Born and raised in Kansas, William Stafford lived most of the last half of his life near Portland, Oregon, where he taught college. He died in 1993 at the age of seventy-nine. A prolific writer, his process was to write in the early morning before the rest of his family was up. Lower your standards, he would say. That didn't mean he would advise anyone, including himself, to write badly. Stafford meant that, in the midst of creating, all of us should aim foremost to put words on paper. In other words, we'd be best served by getting started, and trusting ourselves.

That's a brief outline of the man, and while I don't love all his poems, I do love a good many. And reading most any of them, even ones that aren't my favorites, inspires me to, yes, start writing. He always made it seem so easy.

So, the William Stafford school.

As a writer—and as a poet—that's meant being open to wherever a piece of writing may take me. As a teacher, that's meant being open to all kinds of students and sharing what may take them to the next stage of their development, which necessarily varies by student. I think here of advice I recently offered as a visiting writer on a campus. Your job, I told students, is to not just learn everything you can from your professors in class, but to learn more than that. It's your right to ask them to closely read and reread your work, answer questions, advise you on all manner of issues, and more.

Granted, when I'm a visiting writer, I know full well I'll be gone, and though I invite students to write me—with the promise I'll write them back—I've learned students will rarely take me up on the offer. That's a shortcoming of theirs, but one I understand. Though I explain how I can be helpful in various ways—if I get to know their work well enough, I would some day be able to write letters in their behalf—it all can seem too vague. After all, I'm only a visitor, and no celebrity. Still, for however long I'm around, it's my job not only to know individual students so as to better gauge where they are in their development and where they might go, but then be accessible for the follow through. When I teach, the welfare of the student always comes before my own creative work.

I first taught writing as a teaching assistant at the University of Alaska Fairbanks. From the beginning I enjoyed finding ways to trigger students to write more effectively. I held conferences at the beginning, middle, and end of each semester, which allowed me to better know my students. Some students, I found, responded best by keeping a journal; others never kept one, but learned the same lessons in other ways. Some students, I also found, wrote best by turning in multiple drafts, painstakingly revising; others needed the adrenaline of a deadline and wrote their best in that fashion. While stressing the benefits of turning in work on-time, I allowed late papers—though demanded that any late paper needed to come with a written excuse, which would be graded with the same rigor as the original assignment. I learned early on that there were never shortcuts to teaching writing. And that's fine. I don't think I'll ever know how else to teach but by putting in hours and responding to individual needs.

And, as I reread this, I see I've forgotten what's most important: as serious as the writing process and teaching process may be, there better be room for fun. At the end of every semester-long class, I used to always host a party. Now, since I rarely teach in one place for that length of time, I've come to see every workshop or event I facilitate, whether a single two-hour class, a day-long or weekend-long program, or a series of meetings that might stretch over weeks, as a kind of party.

And this book, too, is a kind of party.

Ultimately, if we're not having fun, and not allowing an opportunity to celebrate, what's the point?

For more than thirty years, I've read plenty of books, good and not so good, about writers and writing. And there will always be more of both awaiting. The market is saturated (then again the market is *always* saturated, will *always* be saturated). So why one more?

Part writer's manual (in addition to suggestions and encouragement, there are plenty of prompts), part memoir (about writing, teaching, and reading), part poetry collection (of poems about writers and writing), I've never seen or read one quite like this, which approaches the practice of creative writing, especially the invention of new work, from such angles. There's even a short story. This book is a hybrid work for our hybrid era, a time when more writers have more opportunities, and more challenges, than ever.

I'm reminded how sometimes near the beginning of one of my shows I'll stand on stage and mention there are lots of ways to learn. When I then ask if there's anyone in the audience who wants to learn to play fiddle, I'll invariably see hands shoot up. Then I explain that for people inclined to learn visually, they can learn by watching me play. For ones more aural, they can learn by listening. And for those more poetically inclined, I tell them they can learn by taking to heart the following poem. Then I'll recite "Old-Time Fiddle Lesson," which begins with the lines, "To learn, lock yourself/and your fiddle in a room/all winter, and practice/".

Just as there's no single way to learn to play fiddle, there's no single way to learn to write. I'm happy to have documented what I've learned about the various ways we writers go about our business. Here, I'll ask who wants to be a more productive and self-assured writer. I'm confident any writer or writer-to-be who's paying attention will pick up something of value from the following pages. And so will any writing teacher.

Plus there's a bonus. Who doesn't want to at least check out a party?

Ending this introduction, I'll share two poems.

The first, a sonnet written for William Stafford, is ostensibly about the writing of poems, but could just as well be about any other kind of writing, or about the teaching of writing.

The second is about an actual party for an actual class I taught in Nome. Since I'd been conducting the class over the phone and students were scattered throughout the Bering Straits region, to pull together this particular party took a good bit of ingenuity.

Ingenuity, now that's a quality for writers to cultivate.

And persistence, that's another.

The ending to that second poem refers to a point I'll be repeating: We're all in this together, and if we want the fun, we've got to keep at it.

Bill Stafford

I saw him read one summer in Fairbanks,
the patter between poems itself a poem,
because he was like that, fully at home
with words. That lit June night he offered thanks
for some gladness or other, and laid planks
of language that formed a lucky bridge from
one thought to the next. What might seem to some
a plainness too simple for poetry — drank
of poetry when he spoke. I reflected
for years on his writing, could hear him chime,
sly and instructive, as I connected
with my work. The voice said to make time
each morning, to begin early on task,
to learn from failures, to ask and to ask.

Class Party, Nome

Fourteen people, eight sites,
the semester's final meeting.
From the Nome classroom, I called
attendance, kicked off festivities
by picking an Irish jig, a reel,
a New England hornpipe on mandolin.
Two young women, exchange students
from Magadan, warbled folksongs
in Russian. Next, the three guys
from prison acted a courtroom drama
they'd scripted: *Appeal to God*.
From Wales, Vince blew his harmonica,
strummed guitar, sang Woody Guthrie.
From the Unalakleet Baptist Church,
Loretta played Bach. From Koyuk,
Polly told the story her grandfather
had told on his deathbed. And so on,

until Tammi from Nome counted five, four,
three, two, one, and asked everybody
everywhere to reach for the cookies
she'd mailed late last week, and munch.
It was probably Huey, from jail,
who hammed the comic smacking noises.
I closed by fiddling the waltz in D
I'd written for those who had dropped,
who had earlier dismissed themselves.

1
Icebreaker

Since 1994, I've made my living as a touring artist, sometimes visiting communities solely to do a public show, sometimes specifically to lead a writing or music workshop. More often, I'll lead one or more of those workshops in conjunction with a public event.

When I do lead writing workshops, I arrive early to arrange the room so it feels more inviting. If we're a small group, and there are approximately the right number of chairs around a proper-sized table, great, we're already set. Other times, we have to make the table larger to accommodate more writers, or smaller for less. If I enter a room with a lectern in front, facing neat lines of chairs, I'll drag the lectern to the side, and start putting the chairs in a circle. When offering workshops in theater settings, which occasionally happens, I'll still aim for an informal and friendly atmosphere, even if it's just to remove the lectern from the stage.

It seems obvious, setting up classrooms or meeting rooms in this way, and taking the extra minutes to ensure it. But having sat through sessions where this hasn't been taken care of, I can report that, no, it's not so obvious.

Once we're settled in, I invariably begin by asking participants to get out pen and paper, or computer, or whatever they use to write. There will be seven questions, I say, (though, in my way, I might also say there will be five or six questions, or eight or nine) and you have to answer in fifteen words or less (though if I'm in the mood, I might be even more prescriptive about length and say responses have to be exactly eight, or twelve, or fifteen words). The questions vary, but they might look something like this.

First question: What's your background as a writer?

Second question: What are you currently reading (any favorite authors to share)?

Third question: What's your ideal vacation? (Sometimes, I'll ask something simpler: What did you have for breakfast?)

Fourth question: Who, or what, is the best teacher you've ever had?

Fifth question: Who, or what, is the worst teacher you've ever had?

Sixth question: Who are you, really? (Describe yourself in eight words. You can even think of it as your mini-autobiography, or even your epitaph. If I want to keep the questions more directly related to writing, I'll ask about writing ambitions or dreams.)

Seventh question: What do you most hope to get from this workshop?

After the writing, which only takes a few minutes since the answers are necessarily short and I encourage this writing to be quick and straightforward, we'll go around the room. Later in the workshop, participants will be free to volunteer as much or as little as they want from what they've just written. But for this icebreaker, everyone in the room has to share their name, their answer to the seventh question, and at least one more of their responses.

I share too, of course, and my fifteen-word answer to that last question is usually something along the line of "while I'd like to write something, I'm here facilitating so everyone gets what they want." (My eight-word answer might be "What do you hope to get? I'll help.") Depending on how the group dynamics play out, I'll share first, last, or somewhere in the middle.

Because I put a limit on the number of words, and ask participants to read what they've written without embellishing (though when people have asked if they can add a few extra words to their answers, I'll nod; I may be prescriptive, but always try to stay flexible), we can quickly go through the whole group, even relatively large ones. And because I've asked that seventh question, I have some idea what the participants would like from the session. Some may be looking for inspiration. Others for shortcuts to publication. Others for answers to specific writing-related concerns. Knowing all this instructs me how to proceed. I might then be able to say something in passing that would not ordinarily have occurred to me to share in the context of this workshop, but it's exactly the information that one or more of the participants are seeking. Throughout our meeting, I'm always hopeful I can offer people not only what they already know they want to learn, but also what they most would have wanted, if only they knew.

This icebreaker exercise is useful in other ways.

When I attend a writing workshop, unless the leader is an incredibly good speaker, I'll get restless when there's too much lecturing at the start. Sure, talk can be valuable, and I always want to learn something, but there are numerous ways to go about this. When I'm in charge, we begin by writing, and formally introduce ourselves through the informal sharing of that writing.

I recently led a small workshop in western New York where half of the six participants were high school English teachers. How did I know that? It came from the responses to those initial questions. And knowing that made a difference. So while I may have certain experience and expertise as a writer and as a teacher, I'm hardly the one authority in the room. We're all equals when we begin with a blank page and time to write. Any of us can write something absolutely extraordinary, whether in a miraculous first draft, or through taking an ordinary one, and putting it through a revision process.

And while it's not in my control what writers do outside of the workshop setting, what's in my control is to offer as many resources as I can within the workshop, and offer opinions on how best to use those resources. In a public library meeting room in western New York, three writers immediately bonded because they were also teachers. Meeting fellow writers with the same interests—and same career challenges—certainly qualifies as a resource. If they decide to stay in touch and get together, as I recommended they do, that can well be a benefit weeks and months down the line.

That experience was in contrast to a writing workshop of similar size I recently attended. Perhaps the workshop leader, a celebrated writer, was having a bad day. I'd like to think that would explain it, though, less charitably, I'd suggest the workshop leader just didn't think it was important to take a few minutes in order to learn something about us. As we sat, listened, wrote, and shared, it irritated me that in the two hours we spent together, there was no attempt by the writer to ask any of us who we were and what we hoped to gain from coming. In a different setting, I might have interrupted and asked if we could go around the room and introduce ourselves. But, no, that didn't feel right, usurping the leader's authority. Instead, I participated as felt appropriate, and learned what I could from this particular writer and teacher.

Still, what felt merely awkward early in the session, like a pebble in a shoe, by the end felt like a real distraction, and, for me, a lesson in practicing assertiveness. Why suffer a pebble in a shoe when there's such an easy fix? In retrospect I could have politely introduced myself at some natural break in the workshop, trusting others to do the same. After all, once we get to know one another in settings like this, invariably there will be serendipities, which enrich the experience. People may have recently read the same book, or they live in the same community, or have mutual friends. But without an appropriate opportunity to introduce ourselves, there's no guarantee of the interaction.

Maybe, like the attendees in New York, some of the group are involved in the same kind of work. And while it's not unusual to find high school English teachers among the participants in one of my writing workshops, it's also not unusual to have a high school English teacher, or another writing teacher, named as the worst teacher that participant has ever had. Often, when that happens, I also hear that particular writer had long been discouraged by that experience, and coming to this workshop is a big, brave step in what feels like a tentative return to writing.

I've long thought of these folks, who are returning to writing after a long absence, as wounded writers, and in my experience doing this work I've found there are many wounded writers among us. All it takes is one wrong teacher at one wrong time to effectively silence someone for years, or forever. Even the most enthusiastic and talented writers will find other ways to fill the hours if they're not also confident and committed writers. It doesn't take genius to perceive mistreatment, or develop strategies to avoid it. Enthusiasm and talent are fundamental. But without confidence and commitment, it's easy to quit.

One of my tasks, then, is to not add to any woundings. So even if I'm asking just seven questions, and receiving approximately 100 words of background, those 100 words allow me to better know my workshop participants, at least on the surface. And while I take care not to overplay my role as teacher, I'm just as careful not to underplay. If we're indeed equals in this setting, as I believe we are, it also means I'm foremost among equals. One of my roles is that of timer—during the icebreaker it's my responsibility to quiet someone who goes "off the page" and starts talking in response to one of my questions—so as to ask the next participant to share. It also means, during the course of the session, I might expand one of my own brief answers, and go into more depth if I sense what I have to say is germane to the discussion.

Writing is so very appealing because it's a means to potentially make sense of the universe. There's power in that. It might be a means to redemption. Or knowledge. Or something intrinsic to the individual. And however central writing is in some of our lives, there are those who would like it to be more central.

But with the promise of sense, power, redemption, knowledge, when we share our writing we're risking vulnerability as well as criticism, whether justified or not. Virtually all of us who write, no matter how successfully, have been wounded in the course of doing the work. In my case, while I can point to my experiences and accomplishments — the published poetry collections (and all those poems and stories in literary journals), the memoir, the children's book, the CDs, the public events — I can just as easily point to my frustrations: the three unpublished poetry collections (it should be easier to get additional books published, not harder, so I must have gotten worse at this), the unpublished novel (a failed novelist, that's what I am), the unpublished story collection (a failed fiction writer, that's me), the unpublished sequel to my memoir (this second one is about money, which you'd think would be topical, so I must not have written it very well or gone about marketing it correctly).

It's a hard business, writing and publishing, and, yes, it can be wounding. What's so great about having thirteen books, I sometimes ask myself, when I have six more already written, all of which I believe are worthy, and I can't find publishers for them.

Sure, there's the joy and satisfaction inherent in the process of writing and the completion of new work. But our time on earth is limited, and there are other sources of joy and satisfaction. There's a quote I've heard, which can refer to writing, though I've also heard it used when referring to working in music, dance, theater. To paraphrase: If you can be happy making a living doing anything else, for godsakes go do it, and don't waste your time pursuing a career as a professional artist.

An experienced full-time writer, musician, touring performer, I may be wounded, but I've learned to work around that wounding. Despite the challenges, I remain passionate about the work. And I have to believe that the passion, coupled with the wounding, makes me a better teacher.

Here, I'll point to three of my own worst teachers. If I'd have let any one of them have their way, I can't imagine I would have accomplished what I have, or have continued to teach writing.

Professor A led a writing workshop on Tuesday evenings from 7-10 P.M., my first semester in Fairbanks. Before arriving in town, I'd heard rumors about Professor A's sometimes lackadaisical ways, but those were only rumors, and I wanted to be open to any possibility. Eager to begin my graduate school program, I registered for four classes that first semester, which was an overload, especially when added to my teaching assistantship. Three of the graduate school classes met at night, another on a late afternoon, and my plan was to attend them all the first week. If I felt like I could handle them all, I'd try to do just that. If I needed to drop one, that would be okay too. That first Tuesday night, the day after Labor Day, fourteen of us gathered in a seminar room in the library. Several of us were just beginning the program. Several more were already in the program. Plus there were a few writers from town, taking the class not to satisfy requirements for a program, but to hone skills.

Professor A was clearly unprepared, or, maybe, as I think back, now more than thirty years later, he was drunk or high. Instead of seizing this once-a-semester opportunity to introduce himself and take steps to build a stronger, better writers' community inside the workshop, he shambled through a lecture he'd doubtless given many times before. Lackadaisical, indeed. Instead of making use of his position to prompt fourteen writers to start writing something exciting and new, he dismissed the group two hours early since it was "the first class" and there was nothing to discuss since "we hadn't read anything [for it] prior to the meeting." While he and a group of students adjourned to the campus pub, I drove home to my cabin. The next day I dropped the class, positive I'd benefit more from the other three classes, and that I'd find more suitable workshop leaders in subsequent semesters.

The past thirty years I've met a number of people throughout Alaska who stopped writing after taking one of Professor A's classes. Since I spent the remainder of my time in the program studiously avoiding Professor A, I'll never know first-hand what exactly he did to wound those people. But I can guess. In addition to what I heard was apathetic and erratic teaching, he was infamous for having written twenty-five pages of a novel—a beginning that had earned him a pair of substantial grants—but according to rumor had never progressed past those pages. I'd also heard a decade earlier he'd written and had published a well-received poetry chapbook, but, as far as people knew, hadn't written any poems since.

I remember the summer between my second and third years in the program, when I had friends visit Fairbanks. The evening of July 3rd, four of us went to a bar north of town in Fox, and stayed until 4 A.M. closing. This was in the midst of the bountiful, beautiful Interior Alaska summer—long sunny days going on for weeks, an hour or two of dusk past midnight. Early morning, July 4th, instead of returning to my cabin, we decided to head straight to Manley Hot Springs, more than a hundred miles away, but almost a five-hour trip, the last stretch down a long, narrow gravel road. We'd wanted to soak in the hot springs, and experience a far place.

We arrived exhausted mid morning and found, amid several tents, a flat patch of dirt in the center of the village between the roadhouse and the river. We spread blankets there and napped. We woke at noon, asked around about the hot springs, and took a stroll past several cabins to a greenhouse full of flowers, where 120° water bubbled up in tubs. It smelled tropical, a bizarre little arctic jungle. After a long and pleasant soak, we returned mid afternoon to our blankets, our vehicle, and a lively scene. Perhaps two hundred people had gathered on the banks to drink, carouse, and hurl firecrackers as motorboats roared up and down the river. There was a bar in the roadhouse, and at one point I ventured in to look. That was where I spied Professor A, hunched on a stool, drinking alone, eyes on his highball. When he suddenly looked up, I thought he spotted me, so I nodded a hello, which he didn't acknowledge. Perhaps he was too drunk to recognize me.

Finding Professor A in Manley Hot Springs made me feel as if I'd stumbled upon an expatriate enclave in Mexico, or Morocco. Or, better, an especially remote spot in the Australian bush. Professor A may have wounded a few writers in his time, but now I had a sense of just how wounded, or haunted, he was himself. It didn't excuse him, of course, but at least I could better understand him. I stole out of the roadhouse and back to my friends, glad we could agree to soon head back to Fairbanks. It promised to be a long and rowdy holiday evening in Manley, and I'd already seen enough.

Professor B, meanwhile, was the senior poet on the Fairbanks campus. I'd arrived as a fiction writer and graduated as a fiction writer. But during my three years there the program was so small that the workshops combined genres. That meant poets, fiction writers, non-fiction writers, even the one screenwriter sat around a seminar table to share new work and discuss craft issues. Here, I was impelled to read poetry carefully for the first time, both my classmates' work, and that of the contemporary poets who were influencing them.

On a whim, inspired by my friends' poems, I began writing my own. My classmates encouraged me to write more, so I did. When I showed ten or twelve of these to Professor B, who I hadn't yet taken a class from, the response: "You're a good fiction writer. You're not a poet."

The next two years I wrote a few dozen more poems, including for a pair of Professor B's classes. Professor B offered a number of solid lessons, some of which I'll share later. No, Professor B wasn't so bad, certainly not the worst, but if I had taken the criticism to heart, I'd have dropped the poetry. Later, though my work was eventually tolerated by Professor B, I noted how it was never fully respected.

Two years after graduating from Fairbanks, I landed a full-time job as a visiting assistant professor in Sitka. That year I was invited to lead a writing workshop in a rural Alaska community, where I met a colleague, Professor C. I'd heard this teacher was so tough that in one audioconference class of twelve students, ten had dropped, and of the two remaining students, only one had passed. Professor C was a poet with a first book from a well-respected university press. Since I was in the early stages of putting together my own first book, and since we seemed to have gotten along the weekend I was in town, I asked this colleague for a favor, which was to read the ones I'd assembled, and to respond if there was reason. Professor C nodded consent.

Two weeks later, back at my home post office, noting the return address, I tore open the manila envelope for Professor C's response: pages of red ink and exclamation points, on the last page an explanation that while I seemed to have a good heart and meant well, the work was not good, none of it, and that I needed to "go back to the very beginning." Professor C went on to write that "in order to get where you need to go, I'll have to be a bit tough on you; it behooves me to blow you out of the water here."

I was thirty-four years old then, teaching five classes that semester. Yet I still found time to write prolifically, both poetry and fiction, and had never felt better and more confident about my writing and teaching. I took Professor C's words, pondered them, and vented by complaining to several friends. Two days later, I was back writing. I never spoke to Professor C again, but over the next several months passed along my poems to two other poets with Professor C's credentials or better, and got much more favorable responses. Afterward, I talked at length with one, Professor D, to whom I'd shown the exact manuscript I'd left with Professor C. That writer looked at me, smiled, and said that while Professor C was entitled to an opinion, it was clear that the response wasn't entirely to the work itself, but had to also have been about something else.

I thought about that, and the writing I'd done the past months. What was Professor C's issue? It didn't matter. But what did matter was if I'd been less confident about my work, I might well have shut down after the blistering criticism. And what good would that have done? Instead, it had merely given me pause before I started back up to write more poems, some better, some worse. And as I kept at it, I understood that was the key: to keep writing.

I later met student writers who had encountered Professor C—the shameful Professor C, I want to say—and never wanted to write again. Some teachers, and writers, believe that the writing of poetry—or the writing of any kind of literature—is an exclusive enterprise. Professor C is hardly alone. And it's not just an Alaska thing, where it's the long, dark winters that create a Professor A, a Professor B, a Professor C. It was Flannery O'Connor who once famously declared "Everywhere I go, I'm asked if I think the universities stifle writers. My opinion is that they don't stifle enough of them. There's many a best-seller that could have been prevented by a good teacher."

I'm not interested in stifling best-sellers, or setting up additional roadblocks before writers of any kind. Life is already hard enough. Rather, I want to encourage people who already have an inclination to write, so they'll write more. Writing can be alternately thrilling and difficult, joyful and lonely. Overall, despite the challenges, it can also be one of the most rewarding activities a person can undertake. It's open to anyone with the wherewithal to borrow a pen and find a scrap of paper.

I trust that as writers indeed write more, they'll continue to read, and read differently. And as they continue the process, the writing will grow, and so will they. My mantra is that the more we write, the luckier we seem to get—so on to the next piece. We'd like to write well, but that's not always possible. But what is in our control is to find the time to at least write something. Once we've started, we at least have a chance.

At the end of our icebreaker, a writer will have seven short answers, all on paper. Those are seven potential beginnings, I say. Any one of them can later be expanded, whether through fiction, non-fiction, poetry, a play. And once that process begins, yes, they have a chance.

Anything can happen.

Yes, anything. That's what I tell them if later in the workshop I ask them to take one of those icebreaker answers and to indeed expand.

And that's what I tell them if we don't go back to expanding them before the workshop ends, reminding them that they've still got those several starts, and back home are welcome to revisit them any time.

2
Creating Character: Names from A to Z

I had a best teacher in graduate school, Professor E, a visiting faculty member from whom I took a workshop and seminar the spring semester of my first year on campus. The seminar was titled Teaching Creative Writing and was the most valuable class I've ever had. Thirty-three years later I'm still benefiting.

We met for three hours on Thursday nights and Professor E had arranged a simple, but effective, format. The bulk of each session consisted of two extended writing exercises, led by class members. The theory here was obvious. Since it was a class about learning to teach Creative Writing, we each had a turn leading a writing exercise in a classroom setting. Since we were all writers and teachers, there was the added bonus of not only testing the exercise to see if we'd like to adapt it ourselves for our own classrooms, but also of writing something new in class, which we might share, either within small groups, or to the whole class. Professor E also encouraged us to take those in-class beginnings home, and continue. In class we'd also discuss how to improve on the exercises, and if the talk lagged, Professor E might show us a quick exercise we could teach in five minutes or less. Toward the end of each class period, one of us would pass around a sheet with instructions for that week's homework assignment, which was yet one more writing exercise. Altogether, it meant that every week we'd begin at least two new pieces in class, and begin a third out of class.

During our first class, Professor E gave us an exercise, introducing it with the explanation to choose someone we wanted to visit right now, and write the name atop a blank sheet of paper. It could be a friend, acquaintance, or family member. It could be someone living or dead.

Then Professor E asked questions, beginning with having us briefly describe this person's hands, then this person's hair. The idea wasn't to flesh out the description, so to speak, but to scribble a few words, a quick sketch. Professor E asked us to name an object associated with this person and to imagine where exactly we "saw" this person. There were perhaps ten questions in all for what Professor E called "A Portrait in Words." Afterward, Professor E gave us fifteen minutes to expand on what we wrote. I don't remember who I chose to write about, but recall that many of my classmates had more success with this exercise than I had. What I'd written hadn't satisfied. Something about the exercise rankled me.

As the semester continued, I had promising beginnings for many of the writing exercises from that class. Some of these I expanded and submitted for the writing workshop. Others I saved to expand and revise for when I had the time. But I never did anything with Professor E's "Portrait in Words" until after I graduated, and stumbled on a way to adapt it for my own creative writing classes. Years later, it's become one of my favorites.

I begin by writing a name on a board, though even if there is no board or easel, we proceed by having all of us write the name I say aloud. It might be Ann (or Anne—the Anns and Annes I've known haven't appreciated having their first names misspelled, even when it's an understandable error), Alex, Andrew, Arthur, or Abby. Then I might write Bob, Benjamin, Betsy, Brian, or Barb. And then

Clyde, Cornelia, Cooper, or Candy. And then I'll stand poised, patient. If no one says anything, I might wait longer, or else decide to get on with it, and say David, or Daisy, or Dee, and write the name down. Then I'll stand there waiting for someone to call out Elizabeth or Evan or another name in the sequence. Eventually it gets rolling, and the naming of names is part of the fun. Everybody can do this, and we might have a list that goes: Anne, Brian, Cooper, Dee, Evan, Franklin, George, Harriet, Ichabod, Josie, Keith, Lisa, Meyer, Nicholas, Olive, Pam, Quint, Rocky, Slim, Terry, Ursula, Viv, Wendy, Xavier, Yolanda, Zeke.

In most classes, the enthusiasm builds as we go down the alphabet, and there's also the mystery: what are we going to do with the list. At the end, I'll ask whether we've indeed listed 26 names. I'll watch as the class nods.

Yes and no, I'll answer. There are 26. And there are more.

More? The class sees the list of names. What else can it be but 26?

I'll go on that just like Ann and Anne are different names (if we even have that discussion), Ursula is different than Ursula Cooper, or Ursula Yolanda Cooper, and both Ursula Cooper and Ursula Yolanda Cooper are already up there, just waiting for someone to notice. As is Slim Terry. As is Lisa Meyer. So while there are 26 first names to choose from, there are many more if you couple a first name with a last name (since there are inevitably first names that can double as last names), or decide a proper first name, middle name, and last name.

Perhaps it's an arcane point, but it indicates specifics, and writing is all about specifics. From there it leads into what I borrow from Professor E. After I ask attendees to write down a name that appeals to them in some way from the list, a name which they can live with for the next stretch of time, I ask up to a dozen questions about this "person," or, rather, character.

While I might follow Professor E's prompts about

describing the character's hands and hair, because they're good neutral ways into the exercise, I let my intuition and experience guide me. Like Professor E, if I do ask about hands, I'll ask if the hands are large or small, dirty or clean, long and painted fingernails, or ones that have been chewed on. Is there a scar? Jewelry?

As for hair, is it curly or straight, long or short, dark-colored or lighter? Is the person wearing a cap, or a wig? And for the contrarians out there, I point out that, sure, maybe the person is bald.

Again, I can't emphasize enough that the idea is to just jot a few words or a phrase, not to strive for anything more polished. And while I may ask about hands and hair, I can also ask about teeth or feet. And over the years, as I've continued to use this exercise, I've learned I can take it in any number of directions. I might ask to describe this person's favorite piece of clothing, or favorite t-shirt. I might say how this person has a doctor's appointment the following day—what's it about?

Or I might say that this person didn't sleep well last night—why?

Or that this person has had a recurring dream—what?

Or I might ask what is this person's usual breakfast, or lunch, or dinner.

Or what is this person's favorite place, or whether this person has a pet, or a pet peeve.

Of course the possibilities are endless, and I mention this as I toss questions out there for the writers to consider for their characters. After I ask my eight or nine or ten questions, I'll ask one more: take one of the previous answers and expand in some way. Afterward, I'll often say that while we might have only fifteen or twenty minutes now, you might end up taking a few hours or days to turn this into a more fully realized poem or story. Or a few days, weeks, or months to turn this into an even more realized story or poem. Or, who knows, maybe you'll take a few years, and turn this into a novel.

Then again, you might have gotten lucky, felt you've "finished," and already turned this into something publishable. Here's a poem of mine, written in response to this exercise, which I'll sometimes share. You can see where I came up with the title:

Frank Leopold, Jr.

Mostly he wishes his dad wasn't
redneck bastard, his mom wasn't useless,
his stupid life wasn't criss-crossed
with grief for losses he couldn't name,
wishes he could accept the long fingers
that ought to be stubs, the big red curls
that ought to be shorn, days and nights
that cry dry storms. Recently busted
at work for downloading porn,
he wishes that nothing and everything could
change, this dusty spring could be
the same as his recurring dream:
riding his bike in front of a speedy truck,
somehow flying over traffic unharmed.
Frank Leopold Jr., age twenty-three,
decides to reopen the book
he's just set down. And so begins
Crime and Punishment for the fourth time.

While all of us can teach—after all, what's teaching other than, literally, showing somebody how to do something—some of us do it more naturally. Some years ago, mulling a return to more formal university teaching jobs, I'd written in application letters that I was "a teacher," explaining that while I hadn't had a full-time teaching position since the early 90's, almost everywhere I went, I was either introducing people to poetry, or traditional music, or Alaska, or sharing more deeply in classrooms. In addition to leading writing workshops, which included both poetry and prose, I've also led workshops on how to live a writers'/artists' life, which means how to live more creatively and productively.

This knack for teaching didn't happen by accident, though chance played a part.

I grew up playing tennis, lucky to have found my sport at an early age. My father had played in high school, but hadn't continued. My mother knew nothing about it. I played every sport I could, then attended a day camp, where I was introduced to tennis, and after a few lessons was hooked. Going on to play regional tournaments, and occasionally national ones, I was consistently ranked near the very top of my age group in the region, and the talent opened doors. Until a series of injuries, I played at college, and after my freshman year I spent the summer near Philadelphia with my parents, and taught at a tennis camp run by one of the pros who had taught me. The next five summers I taught at a tennis camp near Boston, where I worked with a variety of age levels and abilities, both children and adults. Sometimes I taught groups; sometimes, privately.

I knew the sport, so had the knowledge. More importantly, I had an aptitude for connecting with whomever was across the net from me, instinctively knowing when to push, when to take it easier, when to stop and explain, when to shut my mouth and keep feeding balls. The following decade I occasionally taught tennis in North Carolina, Washington state, and in Alaska (the perfect summer job to help me survive graduate school).

I've already mentioned that in graduate school I was a teaching assistant, which meant that over three years, each semester I had full responsibility to teach either a freshman composition class, or one in remedial English. That added up to six writing classes. In addition, over that same period, I led an ongoing Creative Writing workshop at the prison in town, and also taught two remedial writing classes there through the local community college.

By the time I'd graduated, I'd taught eight college-level classes and had led a long-term writing workshop. By taking the required classes, I'd not only experienced Professor A (if for only a single class session), Professor B, and Professor E, but also others in the department, including some who'd studied writing theory in depth. We'd also been required to take a class in teaching composition, so I'd read widely in the field. I saw first-hand what worked, what didn't, and how teachers could adapt.

As I grew surer of my own writing process and pondered how others went about theirs, I found I could transfer the strengths of my tennis teaching to the teaching of writing. Just as every tennis player learned at their own rate in their own way, so too did every student writer. It may have been time-consuming to manage three rounds of student conferences in order to individually meet with every student at the beginning, middle, and end of every semester, but I did, and didn't see how to more efficiently gauge my students' interests and needs. It was like the private lessons, an opportunity to do so much more in a limited amount of time.

I didn't see how else to teach writing but by assigning papers that had a real purpose, and were open-ended enough so students could find topics that truly engaged them, and which I would read carefully and respond to at length and in depth.

Of course, I wasn't perfect—no one is!—but I had success with how I went about this. And to this day, those short questions I ask at the beginning of a workshop are an attempt to get to know who I'm meeting in order to better share my expertise. And when I'm in a setting where I have the names and contact information for my attendees ahead of time, I'll introduce myself a few weeks before our scheduled meeting, and send along the questions.

Of course, there's never one way to write, or to teach writing. By reading interviews with acclaimed writers,

I've learned how writers have succeeded using completely opposite paths. Some will swear that they need to outline meticulously before starting a project. Others will claim that outlining a project will kill their interest. Some write in the morning; others at night. Some insist on coffee; others on alcohol; others abstain from all beverages. Alex Haley, author of *Roots*, used to book passage on freighters that sailed for months at a time. Free of distractions, committed to a period of enforced timelessness, he was able to write more productively. Georges Simenon, prolific French author, would see a doctor prior to beginning a new book, then sequester himself in a hotel room to race through the writing in a few weeks, checking in with his doctor again upon re-emerging after the completion of yet another manuscript. Others, like William Stafford, who I mentioned in the introduction, woke early to write downstairs while the rest of his family slept, and before he had to begin his familial and professorial responsibilities.

Similarly, I find some writers will respond best by having specific writers to read or model. Others by keeping a journal, perhaps even by keeping a journal of letters, which they may send, or not. And others profit by getting started on a single piece, and taking it through revision after revision.

Again, there's no single way, and the better teachers don't just assign and respond formulaically, but trigger apprentice writers to begin new pieces that truly excite them, so it's their own writing that inspires them. The better teachers more freely share resources (and understand that resources are everywhere, so the great challenge is to cut through the chaff in order to match specific resources to specific writers).

Ultimately, there's no single approach; there's never one way. After a point, it's up to a teacher to offer an appropriate overview, and then get out of the way once an individual writer realizes that ultimately it's up to him or her. Over time, upon better knowing a student, a

Writing Party / 27

teacher will know when to more specifically prescribe. But until then, the best way to go about this is to share as much information as appropriate, stay present and available, and to encourage everyone to keep writing.

3
The Dictionary Game

Any piece of writing, I might say as I stand in front of a writing workshop classroom, is made up of words. There's no way around it. And *this*, I say, brandishing a dictionary to the group, is quite a book. Then I shake that dictionary (vigorously shaking a big hardback dictionary is part of the theater here, though any paperback dictionary, or even a thesaurus, will do), and place that shaken book in front of one of the participants.

Open it, I say.

The participant will do just that, some with a flourish, taking my exaggerated shake of the dictionary as cue. Others will be more reticent. If they open it to, say, somewhere in the middle, I might see words in bold on top of the page: *mill, mind, minded, minor*—all good words, I say, after reading them aloud—and then I scan the four columns on the two open pages, and mention some of the words that now, as I read them there, have suddenly come into my consciousness: *millennium, million, millionaire, mime, mimic, mineral, mingle, miniskirt, minister*. More good words, I say, and I choose one—let's say *million*. Then I shake the dictionary and put it down in front of the next participant.

Perhaps that writer will open to near the back of the dictionary. We'll go through the same process: in bold at the top are *trimming, tripodal, tripoli, trochlea* (which, by referring down, I see is literally a block or a pulley, though is also defined as a part of our anatomy which functions like a pulley; by the way, when choosing words from the dictionary, the idea is to take more common words, not obscure ones, though if someone chooses something esoteric, well, that becomes part of the lesson), and on the two pages I find words like *trimonthly, Trinity, trio, trip, triple, triptych, trite, triumph, trivia*. And this time around, let's say I settle on *triumph*.

The next participant, picking a page from near the beginning, might open the page to this: *bacchic, bacteriophage, bacteriophagic, bake*, which leads to a list which includes *bachelor, back, background, bacteria, bag, baggage, bagpipe, bail, bait, bake*. Here, why not, let's go with *baggage*.

So, to begin with, we'd have three words on a board: *million, triumph, baggage* (though one variation of this would include multiple words from each page—and there are always near-infinite variations on how we go about this). Depending on the size of the group, I'll go around the whole room once, where I shake the dictionary for each person, who opens the book, and I choose a word, and then a second time, where the various participants both shake and choose. Part of the fun is the ritual. But what's practical is we now have a list of words we didn't have before.

Even a single word like *million, triumph,* or *baggage* can be a useful prompt. But it can be more fun to combine the words to have *a million triumphs* or *a triumph that is the result of a half-million steps* or maybe the writer will want to focus on *baggage*, and how *in the end we carry baggage, all of us, and despite the challenges, the millions of things that go wrong every day, we make it through, and that's a triumph*.

Or if we're inclined to poetry, we can go in this direction:

Lost Baggage

She had smoked
a million cigarettes,
then stopped.
She loved him.

He had flirted with
a million women,
then stopped.
He loved her.

They had argued
a million times,
then stopped.
They loved

each other.
It's a triumph,
losing bags
this way.

    No, this may not be a publishable poem (although I think we'll agree that we've read worse), but it's something (and something only written because I had three words and gave myself reason—and several minutes—to use them).
    And if we go around and have a list of fifteen or twenty words, there are more options, and potentially more fun to be had. The idea isn't to force things. A single word can propel a writer to action. Using two or three can nudge a poem or story in a surprising direction. Show-offs like to use every word listed, and that's fine. After all, it's only practice. Still, it's the more skilled writers—often the show-offs—who use the words so casually it's as if the prompt hadn't existed.
    And how to become more skilled?
    Repeat after me: Practice.

Again, every exercise can be used in any number of ways. For instance, I can take the generated list as a prompt for the participants to come up with titles. Three words aren't much in this case, but with a little tweaking—always permitted!—we can use a couple of the words at a time to come up with *The Millionth Triumph*, or *A Million (with Baggage)*, or *His Baggage: Her Triumph*, or else use just one of the words, so we might have *A Million Miles From Earth*, or *Bag or Baggage*, or *Grandma's Triumph*. From there, the whole group can vote on a favorite title. When we've decided on one, the whole group will then write individual pieces that start with that identical, consensus title.

I used the exercises in Professor E's class my second semester in Fairbanks as a beginning for most of the stories and a few of the poems I'd write over the next two years. In fact, the whole graduate school experience was invaluable for giving me time and space to explore my own burgeoning writing process. It helped that I lived alone and without a phone in a cabin in woods far enough from campus in one direction, and town in another, so I didn't go out on a whim. Of course, the climate factored in. A high temperature of twenty below zero was not atypical in Fairbanks from November through February, and it took work to get my older vehicle warmed up and ready to go. I rarely had Friday responsibilities, so, with a refrigerator of food, I learned to hunker in from Thursday evening until I had to head back to school on Monday. With three full days to read and write, I found I could do most of my coming week's assignments, including drafting a 5-to-10-page short story.

This was early 1986, and while most all of my professors and classmates had computers, I didn't. Though I hadn't written much prior to attending graduate school, at least I'd written a few pieces of sufficient quality to admit me into the program. But the demands of Creative

Writing graduate school were something different. I'd write first drafts by hand, quickly filling blank white sheets, then refer to that as I expanded into a second draft, and then a third, all in my barely legible scrawl. It may have been laborious, but it worked. By the time I transferred the work to the blank sheets that I set into my portable electric typewriter, and started pounding on the keys, I was almost there. I'd usually type it through once, let it sit, then retype one more time. I became expert in using white-out to erase the more flagrant typos.

Sometime during the summer of 1987, a friend convinced me to buy a computer, since in the coming six months I'd have to complete my thesis. That final year in Fairbanks, I still wrote multiple drafts longhand, but abandoned the typewriter for my new computer keyboard and its word processing capabilities. This transition had come at an ideal time. Almost all the new stories I wrote my last Fairbanks winter had gotten their start two years earlier in Professor E's class. The extended period between idea and execution had allowed the beginnings to properly gestate. These later stories were all longer, more sophisticated, and stretched from 15-to-20 pages. When making some of the changes recommended by my thesis committee, it was a relief not to have to retype the whole manuscript.

After finishing my MFA program, unwilling to leave Alaska, but feeling I needed to leave Fairbanks, which I loved, but thought might stunt my growth as a writer, I applied for college teaching jobs throughout the state. Unable to land one, I moved to Juneau, the state capital. Within two months I fashioned a life where I taught tennis at an indoor health club, taught community creative writing classes, taught fiddle classes, and also taught a statewide developmental writing class by phone as an adjunct through an office out of the Fairbanks campus. That same year I lived in a cabin on Douglas Island, across the channel from Juneau, and it felt luxurious to stay home and teach over the phone, and in the next days have assigned papers from across Alaska delivered by the postal service to the mailbox at the bottom of the driveway.

I saved enough money my first four months to quit teaching tennis. It was a stretch financially, but rent was minimal, and my monthly student loan bills, which had just started to kick in, were manageable. I lived frugally, and used the time to continue writing the short story collection that been my graduate school thesis. I also was composing more poems, happy to have discovered the genre. Sometimes I only had a few hours, and it was a revelation to see how sometimes in the space of one or two sentences, with a few smart line breaks, I could complete something satisfying, ambitious even. There was something to this poetry, more than I realized in graduate school, even with input of professors and classmates, so I began my own personal poetry self-study. I read poems where I could find them, whether in literary journals, anthologies, or full-length collections. Of course I knew how to use the library. I read essays on craft, and interviews with poets. When I had an hour or two, and the impulse to write, but didn't know where to start, I'd go to the dictionary, shake it, open it, and choose a word, sometimes purposely not choosing the word I'd ordinarily choose, but a word I'd imagine selected by someone in one of my workshops. Then I'd shake the book again and again, choose more words, and start writing guided by the list on the top of the page.

That year in Juneau I realized that writing was a matter of choice, and a writing practice was not intrinsically better or worse than any other practice. Playing a music instrument, gardening, hiking, climbing, cooking, inventing, building—they were all worthy if they involved you fully, and allowed you at some level to grow further into yourself. In Juneau I felt lucky to practice both writing and fiddle playing. And as I continued writing poems, I found the traditional music I played appeared in the lines more and more.

The poet and writer Robert Bly wrote something I've often paraphrased. If you want to learn to write, Bly explained, don't take writing classes; rather, apprentice yourself to a master in a field that interests you. By doing so, Bly went on to say, you'll understand what it takes to become a master—and to write you simply transfer those skills and integrate them to the practice of writing. As an added benefit, the apprentice writer will be privy to a whole set of stories that can only be obtained through putting time in this other field, and will also have learned the vocabulary of the particular field, which makes for more effective storytelling. Bly concluded that this wouldn't be done in a traditional writing classroom.

And that's true enough, up to a point, and it leads to the ongoing argument whether we can, indeed, teach writing—and whether there's value in getting an MFA and then a PhD—or whether writing is an innate talent that can't be taught and is best developed individually.

Though I'm a graduate of one of the older programs—the Creative Writing MFA at University of Alaska Fairbanks was founded by University of Iowa workshop graduate and poet Edmund Skellings in 1963, long before the recent rise of programs—it's not only on the periphery geographically, but it's on the periphery of the field. It's never been considered a top-flight writing school, and is never mentioned in the top 50 or 75 programs, some of which now have only been around for a decade or two. The school is rarely spoken of except as a novelty—much in the same way Alaska is so often spoken of—although, to be fair, while it's invariably somewhere near the bottom of any ranking of programs, I've also seen it listed in the past as "underrated."

It would be easy for me to pile on, and talk about why its poor reputation is deserved, and why Bly is correct in that we hardly need writing classes in order to write. Though I thoroughly enjoyed Professor E and learned much in the two classes I took, Professor E was only there my first year. Over three years I received absolutely nothing from Professor A. And while I learned several valuable lessons from Professor B, a fine poet, to this day I still believe Professor B thinks I should never have strayed from writing prose (and maybe Professor B was right—I should have stuck to the fiction writing—though I've somehow managed). What's certainly true is I never did find a mentor in Fairbanks, and have long gone elsewhere for professional references. Despite success getting published, and plenty of invitations to visit campuses where I had little or no prior relationship, I've yet to be asked back by the department at my own graduate program, though I've queried for years now.

What I mean to say is that as a marginalized graduate from a marginalized program, I have an unusual perspective from which to view the whole Creative Writing industry: the pros and cons of various programs; the issues with residency and low-residency programs; the choices between going to school or forging onward through a mix of self-study, an occasional conference or residency, tenacious persistence. I've tried most everything myself at one time or other, and remain curious about the process.

And, of course, as I continue with my writing, my teaching, my reading, it's obvious there's never one answer to any of this. By god, experts in all fields invariably disagree, often bitterly. So it always comes down to individual cases and the answer is the old stand-by: it depends.

When I arrived in Fairbanks, three months before my 30th birthday, I'd written a half dozen short stories, including one several months before that far surpassed the others. I didn't know exactly how I'd done it, but I had, and, more importantly, having written that one, knew if I set up my life in certain ways, I could tap into what allowed me to write than one in order to write more. On the strength of that story, I decided to apply to a single graduate school in the Interior of Alaska, and sent it in with a pair of earlier pieces.

I was accepted. Though I'd read a fair bit of contemporary fiction the past decade, had worked in a bookstore for eighteen months, and had taken a pair of writing workshops as an undergraduate plus two literature electives, my undergraduate degree was in Management Science. Maybe I could write a successful story. Maybe I was confident I could write more. But I was ignorant about both the actual craft of prose writing and about the tradition I was seeking to somehow join.

I graduated with an MFA three years later having written another eighteen stories, my first thirty poems, a few dozen essays and critical papers for various theoretical, pedagogical, and literature classes. I read for a comprehensive exam in fiction (which I passed only after failing the first time). I gained teaching experience.

And while I might not have practiced Bly's dictum to learn another trade and translate it to writing (unless you were to count the tennis, or the fiddle), I did learn enough about Interior Alaska to know I wasn't ready to leave the state, so moved to Juneau, which led to the year in Sitka (the year I encountered Professor C), two years in Nome, more time in Juneau, and then a stretch in Anchorage. I've written a great deal about living in Alaska, and to this day talk about it on stage during my shows. Though rarely in state now, I still identify myself as Alaskan.

Sure, much of the teaching I received in my graduate program in Fairbanks might have been indifferent, and those years visiting writers rarely came through so there were few networking opportunities. But, again, I greatly benefited from the year Professor E was on campus. And I remember what another year-long replacement visitor, Professor F, told me about the Creative Writing workshop process: If a single reader said a single thing that resonated, made you pause and think of your writing differently, allowed you to make changes sooner than you would have otherwise, that single comment more than made up for all the rest, which you could ignore.

Of course I found people, mostly fellow students, who said a few things that helped me on my way.

Most of all, I found a place that suited me. Maybe I got lucky. I loved Fairbanks from the start. Though my arrival in early August was a good six weeks past summer solstice, the big sky and the last of the season's long days thrilled me. The relentless six-month winter was perfect counterpoint, prodding me to stay indoors for long weekends and write. The school may have had its faults, but I was happy to be mostly left alone, provided with just enough structure, and reasonable enough goals. As I sailed through my three years there, I found my way to enough resources to allow me to continue to grow as a writer.

My experience may have been uneven, but I left not only with a degree, but with all that new writing, and a means to keep producing.

So, can you actually learn to write in one of these programs?

Or is writing an innate talent that can best be developed individually (without the need—and expense—of formal writing classes)?

Those may be the obvious questions, but there are other, maybe better ones.

Where can any of us find time to write, and a community of writers to write and read along with us? And if writing is indeed an innate talent—and wouldn't we all have it, since, after all, it's just the process of putting language, which we all use, in a format so others can read it—how can we nurture that talent?

We may not all have the same potential, but I've long heard it's not the potential, or the talent, that makes someone a writer. Ask the people in Iowa City: it's the practice.

I arrived in Fairbanks determined to write a novel

that thirty-four years later I *still* haven't written. Who knows, if I hadn't done the program, or had done it differently somehow, maybe I would have written the novel during those years. Indeed, maybe it would have been "a success," and would have catapulted me to a "successful" writing career (and isn't that, secretly, or not-so-secretly, what I've wanted all along—to write one or more books that are recognized, respected, and read by a discerning audience, and for which I'm justly compensated).

Or maybe by writing that novel "unsuccessfully," I would have learned enough to then write another that would have been "successful."

But I've learned enough to know that publication would have been a longshot, even if I had written the book then, and executed it to the best of my ability. And who's to ever say what would have happened next. Thinking like that can be crazy-making.

I have a friend, Scott, who started a novel in the mid 80's, when we were both living in Seattle. I remember reading a draft in the early 90's, and it certainly seemed publishable then. Scott never went to a writing school, and for years occasionally labored on the novel as he married, moved, worked an advertising job, and, with his wife, raised a son. Every few years he might attend a conference, or join a local writing group. Through a series of happy accidents, in 2010 his often-rejected novel got in the hands of an editor at a highly-regarded independent press, who found it wonderful, and published it in summer 2011.

The book received a starred review in *Publisher's Weekly*, and a good bit of positive notice locally, regionally, and nationally. That's more than most of us will ever get. Still, according to Scott, the book didn't sell as he hoped. The more we get, the more we want. He's working hard on the next one now. I've watched from a distance, glad my friend finally got his book in print, sad that for whatever reason his work didn't receive more attention.

Perhaps if Scott had attended writing school, the manuscript would have found a publisher more quickly. Perhaps not. Or if he'd have attended writing school, he'd have his MFA, a credential that would allow him to more easily supplement his income with teaching writing workshops and long-term visiting writer jobs. While Scott earns reasonable money at his advertising job, I know he'd love to give it up so he could live wholly as a practicing writer, doing some teaching, including semester-long or year-long jobs. But there are always trade-offs, and this kind of thinking, too, gets crazy-making.

In the end, we have twenty-four hours every day. We spend time eating and sleeping. We spend time working, and if we're writers, we're lucky if we can somehow make our own writing a central part of that work. For many of us, the writing comes only after a full day at another job and after we spend time with family or friends.

And if writing comes after the day job, and after family responsibilities, that's going to be a challenge.

How does any of us make time to write?

Okay, maybe you're not going to actually learn to write in graduate school. Still, it's a place to make writing central to your life. It can give you a chance, like it did for me. When I look back to the 12-15 writers whose time going through the program overlapped with mine, as a group we've had mixed results. Thirty years ago, one classmate made a connection at a summer conference on campus that led to help finding a publisher. The resulting book, which was highly praised, had been written under the close guidance of faculty while in the program, and led to several awards, and a tenure track job, which then led to tenure at a university with an established writing program. Attending our out-of-the-way MFA program made that happen. Another classmate also published a book, and on the strength of the work was later named writer laureate of Alaska—surely the MFA credential, and the resulting connections, helped make that happen. Another classmate, a year ahead of me, published a guidebook twenty-five years ago; another, two years behind me, came out with a memoir. The others, as far as I know, stopped writing poetry, fiction, and creative nonfiction, or at least stopped sending the work out. Others from the community who took workshops while I was there have had success. At least three went on to publish books, one to great acclaim.

Graduates preceding my time and following my time probably have similar percentages—I don't know since, again, the program has not been one to foster camaraderie among alumni. Me, I just go about my business, which includes keeping somewhat current in the field.

So, no, you don't have to attend a writing school to become a writer, but attending, and graduating, can help with drafting, revising, publishing, and finding jobs.

And for those who worry, or complain, that all writers attending programs end up writing the same "MFA stories" or "MFA poems," thereby impoverishing contemporary American literature, I haven't found that the case. While a particular teacher may influence students to write a certain way, there are many teachers going about their business in many ways. An influential teacher is like an influential writer. How many minimalist short story writers followed after the success of Raymond Carver?

Perhaps the rigors of an MFA program—and according to the Association of Writers & Writing Programs guide there are 272 of them out there now—mean the worst of the work rises to familiar mediocrity, which includes timeworn plots, timeworn characters, and timeworn treatments. There are only so many stories out there. But within those stories, there are endless variations, and the better teachers—and there are many "better" teachers—are going to push students to write what only they can write. And there are more and better writing students, coming from most every culture and class, attending these schools to take advantage of these teachers.

Are the stories and poems coming out of these programs the same?

It's no more formulaic than the fiction and nonfiction coming from major New York presses and established independent presses, or poetry that finds publication from recognized presses. Just as some writers will write for certain kinds of the editors and publishers, so too will some apprentice writers write for the approval for a certain kind of teacher. There will always be work that is better and worse, and there will always be people doing original work that is even better than the rest, whether it's quickly recognized or not.

And people judging these things will never fully agree.

At least that's my take, from the far periphery.

4
Occasionally Acrostic, and Other Wordplay

Spring 1992 when I was teaching in Nome, I got sick, an illness time that caused me to take leave of absence and then resign my job as a tenure-track assistant professor. Suffering debilitating and systemic joint pain, I couldn't play music, type, or some days even walk. It's a story I've written about before in depth, though there's always more to any one story.

    I spent a thoroughly awful 1992 summer in Seattle, a strange autumn in New York City, then a slow five months of winter and spring in Arizona. Late May 1993, I returned to Seattle and continued a convalescence routine begun in Arizona. Most mornings I drafted a new poem, then spent the better part of the day revising.

    Autumn 1993 I started sending packets of these new ones to literary journals, and by the end of calendar year had received dozens of acceptances, a much higher percentage than ever before. Some of these newly written poems were set in Nome. Though I'd written about Nome within days of my arrival three summers earlier, now, as I completed more, I realized I had a critical mass of thematically linked poems, enough for the foundation of a unified collection.

One day I made a list of Nome people and places I especially wanted to remember. The next weeks I dipped into that list, crossing out the names as I wrote the pieces. It felt like a home stretch, and I sprinted through the completion of those poems.

In addition to the writing and publishing, part of the healing process was to resume teaching. I began that fall by facilitating a few stand-alone sessions at a church in the Ballard neighborhood. I also started leading weekend-long writing classes at a learning center on Capitol Hill, another Seattle neighborhood.

None of the classes were exceptionally well-attended; I don't think I ever had more than six writers at any time. But there always seemed to be at least two or three, and the time always felt worthwhile. At one session I recalled a prompt given by Professor G, another of the one-year replacement Creative Writing professors I'd met at Fairbanks, who I recalled had once said that to write well meant "saying the unsayable."

Since meeting Professor G more than thirty years ago, I've heard variations of that line numerous times. But what I've never again heard was what Professor G said next: One excellent way to write about love is to not use the word *love* but to use a word that sounds similar, like *glove*, and then to write about a glove in a way that imbues it with love.

The more I'd thought about it, the more the idea appealed to me. And that was related to something Professor E had told us once about a poem that was supposed to end with the line "the heart, that violent organ." But after a typo, the poem now mistakenly ended with the words "the heart, that violet organ."

And according to Professor E, that was where it got interesting. Professor E quickly realized that the poem, which had already explained a violent act, had been improved by that typo, a word that echoed the word *violent*, but turned into something surprising, and somehow right. *Violet* was indeed the better word to describe the heart in that setting; the poem was now made more whole.

Accident?

Sure, I said, relaying the story to the three or four writers who had joined me that afternoon, and then explained that writers were free to use accidents, and everything else, to advantage. Next I offered the class several examples of words that could be similarly confused: *horror and honor, adapt and adopt, marriage and mirage, pain and paint, death and depth.* As an exercise, they could take one of those, or one of those we'd talked about—either *love and glove* or *violent and violet.* Or else they could come up with a pair of their own. I gave them ten to fifteen minutes to write.

I remember how one writer with tears in her eyes shared what she wrote. She'd explained that for as long as she'd been writing, she'd wanted to make sense of having been adopted. And always she'd failed, until just now. She'd always had to adapt, she realized, and the past fifteen minutes, writing furiously about having had to adapt in so many ways, she was finally able to approach what she wanted to say about her childhood and her times as an adopted child. She read tearfully, and proudly.

No, it doesn't always happen as neatly as that. In fact, it rarely does. But that doesn't mean it can't happen. And while I only rarely use that prompt these days—but after writing about it here am now tempted to revisit it in future groups—I'm still intrigued by the exercise and have adapted (adopted?!) it. Perhaps suffering from creeping dyslexia, I've become fascinated by those brief instants where I've caught myself misreading, those milliseconds which link the word that's actually there, and the word I've mistakenly seen. What's going on? One project is an attempt to capture those glimpses.

An example:

Faculty to Faulty

Even when correct,
there's more to it,
teacher. See? You think
you're brilliant. Your
own office, your lounge,
your own bathroom.
Your shelves of books—
some perhaps you've authored—
your diplomas on the wall.
Your colleagues and committees.
Your insurance. Your lunches
and dinners. Your drinks.
Your family. See?
Don't forget your flaws.

    The weekend between Christmas and New Year's that year I offered a writing class. It seemed like a good big-city idea. Surely there were people who wanted to write, didn't have work or family obligations, and could use the time to put proper closure on the old year, and usher in the next.
    Though only two writers had reserved spots, I decided to go ahead with the workshop. Why not? I had my own writing to do, which I'd do no matter the setting. At worst I'd meet two people, share my expertise, and earn a few dollars.
    Friday night, only one of the writers showed up. That was Barbara, who wasn't even from Seattle, but who had thought the idea of an end-of-the-year writing workshop sounded intriguing, so had driven in from the Olympic Peninsula to stay at a friend's. After chatting for several minutes, realizing it might well be just the two of us, we got on with it. We began not by writing, but by continuing our conversation. And so the workshop, at least for that evening, turned into an extended conference, or

private lesson.

Barbara had what seemed an enviable life—single and attractive, she had done well enough professionally to have taken an early retirement from her technology job in Silicon Valley to move to the Northwest, buy a house in a small town known for its arts community, and start a consulting business. She had the time and money to make the change, which also allowed her to pursue other interests, one of which was her long-held dream to write poems. That was what brought her to this weekend-long workshop.

Similarly, I told her my background, how I'd graduated college as a business major, knocked around in my twenties working odd jobs, and started to learn fiddle. When I was 29 years old, living here in Seattle, in the midst of a failed romance, I wrote a story, and immediately knew it was better than anything I'd previously written, and that at that point I was, indeed, a writer. And I knew that while I might not be able to duplicate the strength of that one particular story, I knew I could then write more stories, or, really, anything that came from that same place within.

And it had been true. I'd moved to Fairbanks, gone to graduate school, wrote more and sometimes better stories, had started a novel which I was in the midst of, and had begun writing lots of poems. After Fairbanks, I'd moved to Juneau for a year, where I taught writing workshops, then Sitka where I'd been a visiting assistant professor, then Nome where I'd been an assistant professor. I'd gotten sick, so now was in Seattle, but the past months was writing as much as ever. All poems for now, I said. The past eight years, since my first one, I'd probably written five hundred poems, I added, and had close to a hundred accepted in journals. I was thirty-eight years old.

I noticed Barbara nod throughout. Now, as I write this, I wonder about the situation, which politely could have been called "awkward," and which had the potential for absolute and spectacular failure. What else to expect from a one-on-one weekend-long poetry encounter between a middle-aged man convalescing from a mysterious illness, a healthy middle-aged woman perhaps ten years his senior?

But because it was a weekend-long private lesson, we could invent our own pace. Barbara was smart. She'd read enough poetry to fully understand the gap between what she was aiming for and what she was writing. I could feel her frustration when she read two pieces she brought from home, and then shared what she wrote after our first two prompts. It was true. Whatever the measure, the writing wasn't very good. There were things I could say—that her writing sounded stilted, stiff, too-serious—but that wasn't the point here. She already knew that.

Maybe I'm just not a poet, she mused sometime Saturday afternoon. We were more than halfway through the weekend.

You can do this, I said.

But I'm not, am I, she said.

Not yet, I said. But it's in you. Otherwise you wouldn't be here. I looked at her. You can do this, I repeated.

We talked a lot that weekend, Barbara and I, and wrote only a little. It was unlike any workshop I'd led before or since. Early Sunday afternoon one of the prompts allowed Barbara to write something that was different than what she usually wrote. How or why this was, I ought to remember, but don't. Nor do I remember what she wrote. Only that we'd talked for hours that weekend, spent some time writing, and then she did write something which allowed her to say what she'd been truly wanting to say. As she read that one back to me, she couldn't help smiling. She recognized it immediately, as could I.

What had she written?

It didn't matter what exactly, only that it felt looser,

sounded more playful, was actually "poetic" (but had achieved it by not trying to be). She'd written something that had sounded more like herself. That was the essential step to build on.

Hours later, the workshop officially over, we sat in the classroom, and decided to write one more piece, because that was what writers did. Then we went out to a quiet, but celebratory dinner.

Though I never had Barbara attend another of my workshops, we've stayed in touch. A few years later, for her fiftieth birthday, she had a party and invited me. For the occasion, I wrote her an acrostic poem, that is a poem in a form that spells something down the left side. She told me she liked my poem, which not only spelled her name, but celebrated her writing life. Since then she's attended other workshops, and continued writing. The next years she published work, won several awards, gave readings, and even earned an MFA in Poetry from a low-residency Creative Writing program. She certainly fulfilled her dream to write poems.

Preparations for Turning Fifty

Believe it: when the muse
asks for answers, you must
reply in writing.
Believe it: when the muse
asks for more, you must
return to that writing
and add a voice.

Believe it: when the muse
occupies you, you must
write all that you can. How
else will the muse sing you
necessary and beautiful poems.

Over the years, though my own poetry writing has slowed, I've continued to write occasional poems. Some of those occasional ones are acrostics, though certainly they don't have to be. But what I especially like about acrostics is they take me back to that elemental sense of play (and when I visit elementary schools, I always write at least one acrostic poem for the school). The most basic acrostics with their one-word lines, or obvious and end-stopped messages, may make the form seem too easy or obvious. But what I'll share with students are more sophisticated ones (but still age appropriate) so will usually include enjambed lines and at least approach ambiguity or surprise. Because the poems read well enough from left-to-right, there's a sense that the acrostic is "a secret message" which, when revealed, often elicits oohs and ahhs from students. It's like no acrostic they've ever seen. At best, I'm following the old Emily Dickinson dictum, so am taking the top of their heads off, and am blowing their minds with a poem. And if that first acrostic doesn't do it, I'll often share acrostics using the last letters, as well as double-acrostics, which spell the same word on both the poem's left side and right side.

It's been a useful exercise, writing acrostics. Years ago, when Wings Press publisher, Bryce Milligan, challenged me to write a children's book, I immediately thought of the form, so wrote 26 Alaska-set acrostic poems, going from A-Z. I ruminated on the sequence for a spell, then turned around and wrote another 26. The resulting dos-à-dos book, which I ultimately self-published to go along with my second children's CD, was an immediate success and within months was picked up for distribution by University of Alaska Press.

Hard? Not really. It's a fun exercise, which anyone can try. For that project, I started by making an A-Z list of Alaskan places and terms (of course, X was the great challenge—but I wrote X is for Xmas, then X is for X Marks the Spot), and took it from there, playing with the letters to write age-appropriate poems.

And while I've found acrostics ideal for younger readers—anything to nudge them away from rhyming poems—I've written acrostics that feel as if they've transcended the occasional.

For a recent visit to Culver Academies, a boarding school in Indiana, I was asked to help celebrate a writing awards ceremony, so wrote this double acrostic, which I dedicated to the poetry winner and honorable mentions, and hoped related to concerns:

Culver Questions
for Jamie, Mariah, May

Can you describe that music
underneath a poem? Can you
leave a sorry self alone? Will
voting make you old? Does TV
explore or exploit violence,
real people, freedom, fear?

Quick, your thoughts on Iraq,
ugly babies, drugs. Who are you?
(Everybody better be someone.)
So, tell me a secret (in poems,
truths may not be true—a secret
including). More questions? I
only ask this: What must you do
next to survive, then thrive? In
story or poem, yes, you're the boss.

5
Repetition, Not Rhyme: The Sounds of the Fiddle

Four years ago I was invited to lead a pair of sessions at the Mississippi State Library Conference, the annual meeting of Mississippi librarians. One of those sessions, titled "Making Poetry Fun," sparked a lively debate when I evidently touched a nerve by mentioning that when working with kids, whether in libraries or schools, I consciously avoided sharing rhymed poems. And when leading poetry workshops in those settings, I guided writers away from their obvious rhymes, and toward repetition. And while my own inclination when writing for that audience was to write acrostic poems, I also used as models some of my favorites from Kenneth Koch's book, *Wishes, Lies, and Dreams*, as well as successful poems written by kids in some of my prior workshops. Most of the poems I championed depended on playful (and persistent) repetition, or on sound effects.

But poems are supposed to rhyme, one librarian said firmly, a hand up, and I saw a few others nod, while others looked away. There were perhaps sixty people in the small room, which was packed. People stood milling in the back.

I hadn't meant to be controversial, but as the session attendees leaned forward to see how I'd respond, I thought to myself how poetry can be such a strange bird.

Although it had been a few years, I'd been invited to lead several teacher in-service programs. But those were for middle school and high school language arts teachers. This was something different, a mixed group of librarians of wide interests and experience. I didn't know, and hadn't asked, if the librarians were getting professional development credit, but that didn't seem to be the case. I was here because I'd written a children's book, had a new CD to go with it, and had previously worked successfully in several Mississippi libraries. I'd pitched a session, which had been accepted, explaining how to make library poetry programs fun. And now here I was, facing one of the famous old poetry debates.

Poems *can* rhyme, I said, but they don't have to. These days, the poets I know will only write rhyming poems that are exceptionally subtle. And if they do include other kinds of rhyme, it's to make a point, and in those cases they're doing it more out of irony than anything else.

I stopped, and the room was quiet. I flashed back to graduate school in Creative Writing, where all the teaching assistants shared an office space. Our star poet, Elijah, was a reader for the university's literary journal. Elijah enjoyed making a big deal of bad poems. I can still hear his flamboyant dismissal of rhyming verse: If we can sing it, we don't want it.

But my skeptical librarian was persistent: We're talking about kids. They expect poems to rhyme.

I'd say they expect them to rhyme because that's most all they're getting, I answered. That doesn't mean that poems have to rhyme, or that rhymed poems are intrinsically better or worse, though in my experience many of the rhymed poems they're going to see are so contrived as to be just about unbearable. Besides, I added, since they're going to get rhymed poems in so many other places, as a practicing writer and an experienced reader, the least I can do is give them an alternative.

But I was invited here because I can also play music, I said.

I went to my fiddle case, picked up my fiddle. Listen to this, I said next, then wrapped my left fingers around the fingerboard and plucked the A string several times. People started laughing and the tension in the room eased.

Wait, I said. I have a question. What does that sound like?

And I made the sound again.

Plucking a violin string, someone said.

Ah, I said. A literalist. Any other thoughts?

I made the sound one more time.

A clock, said someone else. A metronome, said another. Water dripping, a voice called out.

All good, I said. There's not one right answer. Then I went to the portable white board and copied the responses I'd gotten to my plucking.

Okay, I said, then picked up my bow, flipped it around, and with its bottom, from down near the frog, knocked one of the edges of the fiddle, so it was wood on wood.

Knocking on a door, someone volunteered.

I wrote that down, then made a dozen other sounds as I went through my peculiar, and practiced, repertoire. I made sounds that may have reminded listeners of an ambulance, of a baby whining, of a haunted house, of a bee, a wasp, a computer game, a burglar going downstairs, a bomb, a crackle of a radio, a pot of popcorn popping, a donkey. It's become my go-to prompt, one that works in theaters, in gyms, in cafetoriums (or whatever they call those part-cafeteria, part-auditorium hybrid spaces), in libraries, and all manner of other settings. It works for audiences of 10, 20, 200, 950. It works for fourth-graders, for middle-schoolers, for AP high-schoolers (and their at-risk cousins). It works in a room of adult workshop attendees, this exercise where I make a series of noises on the fiddle, ask attendees to write what each noise reminds them of (all answers accepted, so if you have no idea, *I don't know* is a perfectly acceptable response), and tell them to keep the piece of paper because we're going to do something with it.

   The origin of this wildly successful writing exercise was humble. I was in Gambell, on the far tip of St. Lawrence Island, where on a clear day it's one of the three places in Alaska where you can actually see Russia. How distant is it? Go to a map and find Nome, which is on the Seward Peninsula, the Bering Sea coast. From there, cross water. You'll find an island, St. Lawrence Island, and two villages, Savoonga and Gambell. Siberian Yup'ik remains the primary language (and Savoonga and Gambell are the only two villages in the region—and in the United States— where the language is even spoken).

   When I taught in Nome, I periodically flew to Gambell and other villages to teach my evening classes by phone in whatever makeshift room happened to be used for college classes. By visiting, at least I had that one session during the semester when I could actually spend time with the students from that village. Afterward, we could visit further, and I'd do what I could to encourage those writers to continue. The next morning, before flying out, I'd usually visit the village school, where I'd play fiddle and lead writing exercises.

   One trip, the Gambell sixth and seventh graders were rowdy. So I made a joke of it with the boy who seemed to be the instigator, walking up to him at his desk, taking my fiddle, and making a horrific noise that sounded like cats screeching.

   Does that sound like torture? I asked. Or is it the sound of nails on a chalkboard?

   I made the horrible sound again, aware for an instant I had quieted the room. The teacher just stood there.

   I drew the bow across strings, making the same awful sound. Somebody laughed, and I turned around, and commanded: No laughing. This is serious, I continued. If you think I'm torturing you, write it down, right now. Torture: T, O, R, T, U, R, E. If you think this sounds like nails on a chalkboard, write that down. If you think this is the sound of a cat screeching or drowning, write it down. Remember, no laughing.

I made the sound one last time.

Write down what you think this sounds like, I repeated.

I'd quieted the group, got most of the kids to write what they thought the sound was like, and decided to make another sound. That worked also. So I made one more. The period ended, but not before a few of the students shared what they'd written.

More than twenty-five years later, the exercise has evolved.

I stood that afternoon in the front of the Mississippi librarians. If this had been an actual professional development session, I'd have asked attendees to write their responses on paper. Instead, here I made sounds, asked for responses, and scrawled them on the whiteboard. When I was through, I had a list, which I read through two or three times. Some of the descriptions may have been interesting enough, but they weren't *that* interesting.

What now?

Sometimes I might read my poem, "Welcome to Nome," where each line begins with the word "where," or read my poem, "Graveyard, Sitka," where each line begins with the word "past," or perhaps read my poem "My Grandfather," where each line begins with the words "My grandfather." Sometimes I'll read a poem by a contemporary poet that makes the same point. But since there were a number of youth librarians here, I went into my bag, dug out Kenneth Koch's anthology of student writing, *Wishes, Lies, and Dreams*, and read a poem that consisted of a girl's list of wishes, each line beginning with the words, "I wish."

With kids, I'll do this a little bit differently, I said, but since we're a general adult audience, if you bear with me, wouldn't you agree that "love" and "death" are two of the great literary themes.

I watched my audience nod.

I smiled then, and said how with younger readers I wouldn't talk about death, but it might be okay here. So, I said, if I can have a volunteer make a request: a love poem or a death poem.

Death, somebody called out. And the group laughed.

And then I again read through the list of words we'd generated from the sounds of my fiddle. But this time, before reading each each new sound, I added the words: "Death is." As I continued down the list, "Death is a clock./Death is a knock on a door./Death is bee./Death is a whining baby." and so on, it was easy to perceive how the repetition added momentum, which had not only made the list of sounds poem-like, but with certain descriptions made for what passed for poetry. Ending with "Death is a donkey" made the group once more laugh.

We went through the list again, substituting "Love is" for "Death is," then alternating the descriptions, "Love is a clock,/Death is a knock on the door./Love is a bee/ Death is a whining baby." There were endless variations, and for the show-offs—and there are always show-offs— there was the option of not writing "Love is" or "Death is" or using repetition of any kind, but to just take the different sounds and stitch them together to make some kind of narrative sense, or narrative *nonsense* if that was in order. And if they wanted to write something that rhymed—skillfully, please!—well, they could try their hand at that too.

The beauty of poetry ultimately was that it was limitless. Though the session's attendees were surprised to later hear me admit to writing plenty of rhymed poetry, I told them I expected I was doing it with skill. I'd taken Elijah's bias to heart, so if I found myself writing rhymes that sounded like something that might be sung, I knew to revise.

Kids were already getting rhymed at in most every direction, I repeated, and explained that part of my life's work has become to show the power in the repetition of words. And to show that making poems is a lot of fun.

After the session ended the librarian who asked about the rhymes came up to shake my hand. She was a writer too, she said, and though she didn't fully agree me, what I'd said had given her something to think about. She asked for additional resource materials, which I was happy to supply.

6
The Poetry Olympics (Yes, Sometimes Poems Definitely Rhyme)

As an assistant professor in Nome, I taught at least four classes every semester, and often taught a fifth. The year before, as a visiting assistant professor in Sitka, I'd taught a similar full-time load. And prior to that I taught writing in Juneau and Fairbanks. The fourteen-week semester could be a grind. But I enjoyed the work, and it fascinated me how to pace classes to best engage so many reluctant readers and writers.

I came to see that my real work in the classroom was to keep things interesting, bide time, and offer as many opportunities as possible until a student came to that "aha" moment, when he or she "got it," "it" being the understanding of what constituted good writing, and what it took to create it.

Some never got closer than the standard refrain: But, teacher, what are you looking for?

My standard response—I'm looking for good writing—only frustrated them. They wanted a foolproof formula, like the five-paragraph essay, but better. That I couldn't give, since my "formula" was a formula that defied formula. By seeking "good writing," I meant I sought honest writing, or fully-engaged writing, or writing that was unique to their own particular writer selves. And those explanations were never going to sit well with students looking for an easy way through.

But students who arrived in a class with that knowledge of what made good writing, or figured that part out—whether in week one, or week fourteen—they were set from that time forward. They'd find that the assignments and prompts gave them flexibility in what to write about. And then they'd get a chance to show how much they knew, and how very smart they really were, which also meant getting to the nitty-gritty gruntwork: the choice of words, and the arrangement of sentences and paragraphs to best explain what they truly wanted to say.

At some point I didn't see a huge difference between a composition class and a Creative Writing class. Ultimately, they were both about first having something to say, then saying it well. Writing wasn't rocket science. Nor was it physics, chemistry, or math. But it was about making sense of things. If they had truly wanted to make that kind of sense, they'd have reason to master the intricacies of language (which, again, wasn't intricate like math or science).

Why mention all this?

Again, I think back to Nome, where I noticed how much the success of both my college composition classes and Creative Writing classes depended on how I set up an exercise, or assignment. Ideally, sure, students ought to be able to just write. And, ideally, writing teachers need only assemble a group, tell the students to write, and then let them at it. Each week the instructor would pick up assigned papers, comment on them, return them, and then repeat the process.

That might have been the ideal. It was also the equivalent of teaching kids to swim by tossing them in a pool.

When I started teaching, I quickly learned never to give the instruction to just free-write, or "write about whatever you want," unless I was prepared to have most of the class scribble aimlessly, if at all. For the majority of students, no matter how many resources I gave them to begin more effectively from scratch, it often came back to another of the standard refrains: Teacher, what are we going to write about?

But if I narrowed the topic—even to something as basic as "write for five minutes about frustration," or "write about your absolutely favorite meal"—there would be traction. The students wrote, and, more often than not, wrote well.

And as I experimented with writing prompts, like first composing the list of names from A-Z, or using the dictionary to make a list of words, the students had even more success.

So, maybe, yes, it was all about the set-up.

Even if every one of us had a reservoir of subjects to write about, we often still needed priming to get started.

In Nome, in addition to teaching four classes a semester over phone, leading a one-credit on-site Creative Writing class in town, and occasionally traveling to villages, once a week I visited a fifth grade class at the local elementary school, and a language arts class at the high school.

The high school was especially rewarding, though as part-visiting artist, part-substitute, I understood I was in a gray space there. How respectfully I'd be treated depended on the week. But since at that time I was so enthusiastic about my writing and music, I usually had good luck engaging with the students. It helped, too, that I brought in some of the poems I was writing about Nome, which they could relate to. I shared sonnets, a form which they were familiar with, and both villanelles and sestinas, which they'd never encountered (which was okay, I explained, since I'd never heard of either kind of poem until I was 30 years old; that was also when I wrote my first poems, I confessed, so they were way ahead of me).

About the villanelles and sestinas, we talked about rules, and about obsessions. Maybe rules could be a problem in real life, I said, and maybe they could also make for problems when writing poems. But if you thought about it more, strict rules could also make things easier. For instance, with a sestina, the same six words had to be repeated in a certain order at the end of six six-line stanzas, and then tied together in a three-line coda. If you chose six words that you really loved, or were somehow obsessed with, well, that could make things kind of fun.

As for a villanelle, it was only about half as long as a sestina, but instead of repeating six words, you had to repeat two whole lines several times in a special order. If you found a couple of lines you liked and somehow could wrangle some sense out of them, there you had it, almost half the poem right there. The challenge was making sense not just with those two lines, but making sense with the whole poem, and to include the rhymes that the form was supposed to observe.

Sonnets? They had already studied them, whether they could remember the defining characteristics or not. We discussed how they had fourteen lines, and rhymed in certain ways. Yes, rhyme. When writing a traditional sonnet, there was no way around certain rules.

Over several weeks of visits, amid other lessons I explained these three forms, and as a group we wrote sestinas, villanelles, and sonnets. We even talked about acrostics. I continued sharing poems I'd been writing about Nome, and each week we spent time composing poetry in class. (With a dictionary alone, there's never a shortage of words for prompts. But I might also conjure up three words—for instance, *color*, *animal*, *machine*—and call for help making lists of colors, animals, machines, and that would quickly lead to a blackboard full of words, and resulting ideas galore.)

One week I smiled to myself when I mentioned that in

a month we'd be holding the Poetry Olympics. When students asked what that meant, I put my right index finger to my lips, and said, Shhhhh. The next weeks I found ways to mention the Poetry Olympics once or twice in the course of the session, but didn't explain further.

Finally, I arrived at the high school one afternoon, and asked who was ready for the Poetry Olympics.

Almost everybody raised their hands.

You sure? I asked.

They nodded.

It's not going to be easy, I said.

They looked at me, waiting.

Since we were in Nome Beltz High School, I wrote the words *Nome Beltz* on the board. Then I wrote ten more words: moose, winter, salmon, ice, light, airplane, moon, Anchorage, basketball, bird.

The Poetry Olympics, I said, is underway. We have 55 more minutes. To compete, you're to write a sestina, a villanelle, a sonnet, and an acrostic in that time. You're to use every one of those twelve words at least once in the course of those four poems. If you finish ahead of time, you're invited to write one more as a victory lap: a free verse poem of exactly 30 words, where you have to write ten three-word lines, and use every one of the twelve words.

Go, I said, and then sat down and started writing with the students.

I knew how every fellow student in my own MFA program, even our star (especially our star), would have balked having to write even a single poem in 55 minutes, much less a poem in a form, much less four or five poems in that time. They would have mutinied.

Here, I didn't know exactly what would happen, but the past weeks I thought I'd done a reasonable job creating some suspense with this. As I surveyed the room, saw one or two writers looking utterly clueless, the rest hard at it, I smiled and then went to work on my own Poetry

Olympics (or, more accurately, a Poetry Pentathlon, I suppose, since a finisher would have completed five poems in the allotted time).

No, the poems didn't have to be publishable, or even "good." But did have to abide by the rules of the forms. I don't remember what I wrote, don't know where that notebook is buried, if it's in my possession at all these days, but managed to scrape my way through the challenge. Having the twelve words on the board helped, though now, more than two decades later, resurrecting the exercise, I only needed the name of the high school to write a super-quick acrostic (though did use another of the words to help with a title):

Not Anchorage

No one knows what's
over the next ridge.
Maybe tundra. Maybe
everything you ever wanted.

Best, then, to go out
exploring this other realm.
Let's go take that hike
to the summit, and beyond.
Zero chance of nothing changing.

Much of the group was still intent writing when the bell rang, the signal to finish up and head to the next class. I quickly asked whether any of them there had finished all five poems.

A few raised their hands.

Almost half had written four. And everyone had written at least one poem.

The next week we shared what we'd written, and it was incredible, really, how good some of those poems were. I told them they had done what not only would have scared off most college and graduate school writers everywhere, but would have scared off most of the professors.

What I'd said didn't matter to this group. They didn't know enough to know what they could or couldn't do. Instead, we'd spent some weeks and had some fun with poems and with a process. There wasn't much more to it than that.

And, really, when it came to prompts, I understood then that it was most definitely about the set-up.

7
Postcards, Anyone?

After graduating college in 1977, I spent the next months teaching tennis near Boston, then traveling throughout the United States with Howard, one of my tennis camp pals. I had several school friends I promised to stay in close touch with, so early in the trip, while Howard and I stayed at his parents' unfurnished south Florida condominium, I got in the habit of buying postcards, which I'd fill with my news, and then send.

Postcards at that time cost nine cents to mail—and a first-class stamp was only thirteen. Since Howard and I were on a budget, postcards felt like a smart value. Having read lots of Kerouac, and having recently discovered Hunter S. Thompson, I fancied myself a Gonzo correspondent, especially since I was writing dramatic reports to friends from my grim all-night convenience store job just off the Florida turnpike. Fueled by bad coffee, my 4 A.M. entries mimicked Thompson's hallucinogen-laced prose. It was great fun to exaggerate desperation, and easy to embrace the postcard's space limitations as I took to writing my friends most nights, sometimes extending a single note over two or three cards. One late night I addressed a postcard to Thompson himself, and the next day mailed it off to Woody Creek, Colorado. Those were heady days.

As Howard and I journeyed to Key West, then New

Orleans, and on to Albuquerque, Taos, and so many other places, I took to the postcards even more deeply. With loads of time and little money, whether in cities, towns, or lonesome western crossroads, I took to stopping in all manner of antique and second-hand shops, where invariably in one of the corners there was a bin of old postcards. While new cards might have sold back then for a nickel or dime, perhaps a quarter, the old ones cost no more, and sometimes went for much less. You could at least offer to buy twenty or thirty for a dollar. And the strange cards were stranger than anything at a regular shop. I'd spend an hour, combing through two or three hundred in order to buy the four or five, or forty or fifty, that most appealed to me, and plunk down a quarter, or a few dollars. Occasionally a proprietor, amused by my folly, would tell me to go back add a few more cards. Evidently the cards weren't the quickest sellers in the store.

After my shopping, I'd buy a beer, chase it with coffee, and when I felt a proper buzz began writing my friends. If we were traveling, the next day we'd detour into a similar shop, where I'd find a similar postcard bin, and thumb through hundreds more.

As I deepened the practice, I realized I now owned cards that felt too precious to send to friends. One day I visited a shop that was going out of business so bought several hundred for five dollars. Learning more about cards, I discovered I'd acquired some collectibles, and when I found more, made sure to buy them when they were priced for considerably less than their worth.

That was also a year I haunted book stores. I spent a sunny November day reading *One Flew Over the Cuckoo's Nest* in an Albuquerque cafe. I read *Tropic of Cancer*, then *Tropic of Capricorn*, then *Sexus*, *Plexus*, and *Nexus* across Arizona and California. I finished my Henry Miller binge while employed as a security guard in San Francisco, but his books weren't always easy to find, especially in used bookshops. If I had known more, I might have taken a side trip to Big Sur. But, no, I didn't know more (nor did I ever make it anywhere near Woody Creek or Aspen when we were in Colorado).

That was the year I started reading George Orwell, Knut Hamsun, Charles Bukowski. Though I had a substantial stockpile of postcards by the time we arrived in San Francisco in late January, I continued scouring the antique shops. When I found postcards I especially liked, I'd add to the collection. I still used them to write to friends.

The following summer I was back to Boston, where I lived for more than a year, spending two more seasons teaching tennis. The winter in between I lived with a girlfriend, took two writing workshops in Cambridge, wrote several stories, and worked a variety of odd jobs. I continued reading, finding my way to Hermann Hesse and Jerzy Kosinski, When my girlfriend left for the Peace Corps and an assignment in The Philippines, I took off for New Mexico, though landed no further than Durham, North Carolina, where I'd gone to college.

A business major who'd taken a few writing and literature classes, I still had friends there, which was fortunate, since it was a rocky time at first. I may have only just turned twenty-four, but my body was knotted up. I couldn't run without straining muscles, which meant I couldn't play or teach tennis, which meant I could only look for menial work. My Duke University B.A. in Management Science didn't translate into practical skills and I worked a string of temporary jobs. A rocky time? It was worse than that. Thanks to the generosity of my father, I was given money to see a therapist.

Later that summer, I managed to pick up a 30-hour/week minimum wage job in a downtown Chapel Hill bookshop. The business was poorly managed and I worked the slow evening shift upstairs in paperbacks. This was summer 1980, the season I first read Raymond Carver and Jayne Ann Phillips. This was when I first read Paul Bowles. One night I leafed through an older collection of stories by the writer, Delmore Schwartz, read "In Dreams Begin Responsibilities" and was stunned, as I'd been stunned by writers before.

I wanted to write something like that title story in which the young narrator had wandered into a movie theater, settled into his seat, looked up with anticipation as the film began, only to recoil in horror. There on the big screen was his father courting his mother — a precursor to everything that would go wrong.

It would be three more years before I took a crack at my version of the story, when I moved to Seattle. But I wrote that story, and then another, something much different, which was the story that told me I was a writer. And a year later, I was in Fairbanks, Alaska.

And through all those moves, from the year of traveling with Howard, to Boston, to Durham and then Chapel Hill, Seattle, Fairbanks, and then the other Alaska communities I lived, to the years touring non-stop, to this day, those postcards have come along with me, at least some of them have. I've lost most sometime during my many moves. Of the ones I still have, a few are ripped. Many are dog-eared. But I still have them, and still use them for writing exercises.

The older elementary school children and middle-school children are especially intrigued. Some of the cards are stamped and postmarked, and over a hundred years old. They not only look old, they feel old, and when I give the students a chance to handle the cards and examine them closely, there's a true sense of awe.

Now, if I were to pass out a card, and ask students to take that card and write about it for five, ten, or fifteen minutes, in most circumstances I'd waste that awe. Instead what I'll often do is take one of Professor E's "two-minute" lessons, which I've adapted. What Professor E asked us to write were lines of 2 syllables, 4 syllables, 6 syllables, 4 syllables, 2 syllables. Now I can count syllables with the best of them, and when I write my sonnets, I'm right there with my 10-syllable lines. But with younger students, and even with my adult writers, I've found it's more useful to have them count words. In fact, I might ask a student to pick a number, any number, between 15 and 20. If the student were to choose 18, I could almost follow Professor E's model, substitute words for syllables, and write on the board:

_____   _____
_____   _____   _____   _____
_____   _____   _____   _____   _____   _____
_____   _____   _____   _____
_____   _____

Though, more likely, instead of the 2-4-6-4-2 scheme above, I would write six lines with three blanks a line, or nine lines with two blanks per line. Even if a student chose a prime number, like 17, I could come up with a new form to fill in the blanks: 4-4-1-4-4 or 2-3-2-3-2-3-2. That part isn't hard. But what makes it fun is the spontaneity, and the proof that anything is possible, and we're inventing it as a group as we go along.

After all these years, even with the losses, I still have a few hundred postcards. These I'll gently shuffle as I ask for a volunteer. When I've chosen one, I turn my head away, ask the volunteer to pick a card, any card, and, after choosing it, have him or her show it to everybody else in the class, but not to me.

The volunteer does so, and then I ask the volunteer for the card, and, if I'm having a little more fun with it that day, will ask the volunteer if we've indeed rehearsed this, or whether the volunteer has ever seen the chosen card before.

After the volunteer hands me the card, I hold it up to everybody, then walk to the board, and fill in the blanks by quickly describing some aspect of the card, which never takes more than a minute.

No, I haven't written anything great. But I've certainly

written something quickly, and successfully modeled the exercise to the group. Then I'll go around the room. Depending on the age of the group and my sense of timing, I'll choose a card for them (with kids it's fun to ask if they want something "normal or strange"), or have them choose a card after I shuffle.

I usually cap this one at somewhere between 15-35 words, enough for a quick exercise. After they write one, if I ask whether they'd like to try another card, the hands will usually shoot up and I walk around to pass another one along. Students invariably find it gets easier to write about this second card, and if they attempt a third it's even easier. And, of course, like the earlier exercises, there are lots of variations. After we're finished, I've found students especially like to share their writing about these, and to explain the old postcards that inspired them.

With writers who are more sophisticated, I don't have to cap the number of words, though I might, and might also be more apt to ask the writers to pick three cards, and to fashion a narrative that might include one, two, or all three of the postcards. The whole postcard is in play here: the front photo, the back description, even the writing if it's one of those postcards that have been through the mail. Sometimes it's even the stamp that's the trigger for the new writing.

With the new technology (and the smart boards, which I'll usually try to dodge), I'll sometimes have one of my more evocative cards on the screen (older elementary-schoolers are partial to the burial ground full of skeletons, but the boy riding the alligator is also good, or the snake charmer playing flute to a snake—I have a lot of them) and ask the whole class to write about the identical card. Again, there are endless variations, and a teacher doesn't need a collection of antique postcards to make this exercise work. A resourceful teacher can buy old *National Geographic* magazines and get to work with scissors, and maybe laminate the photos so they'd be more apt to last beyond a single lesson. Or a teacher can use slides of fine art—and when I've taught on campuses with a gallery, we'd spend at least part of one class outside of class with our notebooks and our pens, taking notes as we walk through an exhibit. *Ekphrasis* is the term for using literature to describe a piece of art.

Postcards like mine no longer go for nickels and dimes—they're more likely a dollar or two each, or more—and there's no way I'd ever replace them at this point. But these days when I take off the rubber band, and watch the reaction of young writers in elementary schools, it's a delight. And for a moment or two, I'm taken back to the year after I graduated college, when I was twenty-two, and everything seemed so fresh. That was the year I found so many new books and writers, the year I collected postcards to help make more sense of it all.

8
The Object Is

One night for Professor E's Thursday night class, a classmate brought in two sacks. In one, the classmate explained, were enough hats for everyone in the class. In the other there were shoes. Our in-class assignment was to dig into the bags for a hat and a shoe, and then let the clothing get you started writing.

For twenty minutes I stared at a white golf visor and a dark-purple high heel before flashing on two characters: a well-dressed woman on a date with her long-suffering partner; and a nameless man, wearing a visor, who takes a seat nearby with his partner. "Black Hair, Purple Lips," is the little four-page story I wrote the following weekend in my Fairbanks cabin.

Black Hair, Purple Lips

"Sylvia, a light?"

"Why thank you, my pet," Sylvia could have said, but instead she gave Alfred a look. Not a look actually, just the slightest curl of a mouth and the briefest flutter of a right eyelid. It said that she not only expected Alfred to light the cigarette, but that he better do it with flair.

Sylvia blew a smoke ring. Then another. The smoke rings had a frail grace to them. They floated across the table, breaking up into Alfred's eyes. Sylvia watched Alfred's eyes water. Silly man, thought Sylvia, as she watched him smile weakly at her. I'm not looking at your eyes. I'm looking at your eyes *water*.

The mirror directly behind Alfred more than doubled Sylvia's pleasure. Not only could she watch Alfred's eyes water, but she could watch herself blow smoke into Alfred's eyes. The scene was perfect.

Sylvia blew another smoke ring, shifted her eyes from the mirror, and watched the ring float and float, and then fade at just the right spot. Then she looked back into the mirror. Her black hair rose up in a wonderfully complex pile of activity on top of her head. She admired, too, how her cigarette fit in her mouth as she smoked. The lips did it, and it was an experiment, this lipstick. The color was the same as her shoes, a pair of expensive grape-colored high heels Alfred had bought for her last month. She smiled at her black dress with its provocative low cut. Her bracelets were fine, but now she felt her earrings and necklace needed more flash, more something.

Sylvia blew one more smoke ring before setting the cigarette in the ashtray. She sipped from her glass of Chardonnay. She looked at Alfred, then the mirror. She saw herself, then beyond herself. She began to stare at what must have been a mistake. Behind her, one table away, a man wearing a golf visor was pulling out a chair and sitting down. His companion, a woman with waist-length blonde hair, wearing a tee-shirt and blue jeans, was pulling out the chair directly behind Sylvia. Looking in the mirror, Sylvia watched her chair get knocked by the woman.

"Sorry," said the woman, who then sat down and maneuvered up to the table.

Sylvia turned in her seat, and gave the back of the woman's head an ugly look. When Sylvia saw that the man wearing the visor was staring at her, she smirked. The man wearing the visor looked at Sylvia's lips for a moment, shook his head, and then looked downward to where her left breast pushed against her black dress. Immediately, Sylvia turned to Alfred, picked up her cigarette, took a furious drag, and blew a thick, low-flying smoke ring that sailed across the table. Sylvia crushed the cigarette in the ashtray. Alfred fished around his vest pocket for a handkerchief, and when he found it, he gently dabbed the moisture from around his eyes.

"The nerve," Sylvia said.

"Nerve?" said Alfred. "What?" He began folding his handkerchief, making sharp, exact creases.

"The nerve," Sylvia repeated. "New money means no class as far as I'm concerned. Put a few dollars in their hands and every place is a pizzeria."

Alfred put the handkerchief back in his vest and stared at his drink. Then he picked it up and sipped. "Sylvia," he said as he swirled the drink in the glass. "Are you saying we should go out for pizza tonight? I thought you decided you wanted to come here for dinner." He nodded to her and smiled thinly as he set down the drink.

Sylvia took out a cigarette and gestured for Alfred to light it. "New money means you come into a nice place like this dressed in the latest of picnic attire. Alfred, this is no picnic ground. A look at the menu and the decor will tell you that." She leaned over and whispered to him. "Let me tell you something, Alfred doll. The man I used to see last summer took me on a picnic. In ninety degree weather we sweltered in a field drinking warm coca-cola and eating soggy tuna fish sandwiches. That's what he called food. And then he put his arm around my shoulder and said we would be each other's dessert. You can imagine how I felt. I was going to vomit and I told him so. And he thought his little picnic was so romantic. Well, I had my own secret treat after he took me home. And I'll tell you, it was no picnic." As Sylvia giggled, she could almost overhear the conversation at the table behind her. She strained to listen, and thought she overhead the word "bitch." She blew a smoke ring.

"What do you mean, no picnic?" asked Alfred, his eyes watering.

"You know, a picnic," said Sylvia, raising her voice so the table behind her could hear. "That informal time for ants and dirt." Sylvia looked into the mirror where she saw the man wearing the visor drinking from a bottle of beer. Sylvia sipped her wine. The man took another gulp of beer. Alfred flecked a particle of dirt off his dinner jacket.

"Yes, dirt," Sylvia said, and as she spoke, she thought she overheard the man wearing the visor say, "whore." She blew a smoke ring. "Going on picnics, drinking kegs of beer, frolicking men and their whores, dancing in mud, studying worms. By god, where does it end? You get dressed for a night out and you find yourself in a middle of a picnic. Alfred, doesn't that bother you?"

"Me?" he shook his head.

"Just look in front of you with your own two eyes." Sylvia took a deep drag and blew. Then she looked into the mirror. There was nothing wrong with the way she looked, and for a second she smiled and saw herself smile. Then she looked farther to see what the man wearing the visor was doing. He was staring at her body, and nodding.

"Alfred, let's go," said Sylvia. "I won't stand

for it a minute longer." She crushed the cigarette in the ashtray, rubbing the gray and blackened tobacco on every surface of the glass.

"Go?" asked Alfred.

"Go," said Sylvia. "To dinner. We've had a drink. Take me somewhere nice for a change. Take me to The Club."

"The Club? But Sylvia, I thought you didn't like the food there."

"We'll try it again," she said. "Maybe they've hired a new chef." As she pushed back to get up from her chair, she thought she overheard the man in the visor say "poodle" and then "leash." She turned to look at him. He was talking to his woman friend. But when he noticed Sylvia staring at him, he stopped talking. His eyes went from Sylvia's shoes, to her hair, to her lips, to her breasts.

His woman friend turned so she could look too.

More than thirty years later now, I've never accumulated enough hats and shoes to exactly duplicate the exercise. But I haven't let that stop me.

A few years ago I led a workshop in Denver with the title: Mirror, Map, and More: An Exploration (and Experiment) with Everyday Objects, Here's how I described the class for prospective attendees:

"One way of defining literature is an attempt to look deeper into what's normally taken for granted. Normally, a mirror is just a mirror. But if you study it, you'll not only see yourself, but see deeper into yourself. Then a mirror might become a door, and a way into a poem or story. Similarly, a map may be a map. But if you study it, you might not only see your home state, or hometown (or a strange state and a strange town), but an entry into virtually any possibility, about making the common uncommon. For this class we'll read a few poems based on objects, beginning with William

Stafford's "What's in My Journal," discuss prose writers from Marcel Proust to Nicholson Baker, and seek ways of taking real note of what's ordinary (and, by honoring ordinariness, attempt to make objects extraordinary)."

Ah, the joys of marketing. Maybe the description was a little too academic-sounding (and, in the ways of these things, maybe not academic-sounding enough). But Lighthouse Writers, the literary center sponsoring the workshop, offers a wide choice of excellent short-term and long-term writing workshops. Attendees may be beginners, but also may already be much-published and award-winning writers. I hoped to make the three-hour session sound like a unique opportunity.

The description must have been sufficiently enticing, because we confirmed eight registrants for a weekday late afternoon class on the Tuesday following Labor Day. When I received the roster, I introduced myself individually to each writer via email, a brief note that closed with three questions and a request. The questions: What was their prior experience with Lighthouse Writers? What was their impetus to take this particular workshop? Who were two or three of their current favorite writers? And the request: Please bring to the workshop a common everyday object.

For my part, in addition to my usual handouts, I brought a small bag filled with various objects I'd dug out of my day pack and pants pockets: battery, cell phone, toothbrush, nail clippers, pen, key, coins, travel clock, paper clips, rubber band, plastic fork. They weren't just rattling around the bag since I'd already wrapped each object individually in its own smaller bag, which I taped shut. I also brought the mirror I'd pulled off from my car's passenger seat sun visor. It felt only right to have a real mirror in proximity—something to pick up and hold. And to see ourselves in, if it came to that.

After in-class introductions, which included sharing what we'd written to my emailed questions, and a brief icebreaker writing exercise, I passed out three sheets:

there was the Stafford poem, there were paragraphs by Nicholson Baker and Marcel Proust. After reading them, we briefly discussed them.

Then I asked everybody to take out the everyday object they'd brought and set it in front of them, explaining that since they'd brought it, now they could own it for the purposes of the writing exercise. We went around with a quick show-and-tell of our personal object. The mirror, which I then set in the middle of the table, was common for all of us. And then I shook my small bag, and we went around the room, each writer putting a hand into the bag, as if picking a tile to see who'd lead off in a game of scrabble. But instead of showing our letters, there was the sound of tape ripping, smaller bags opening, and then the chuckles as we discovered our third object.

The idea, I said, was to take the three objects—the one you brought, the mirror, and the one you picked out of the bag—and write something. There were no other rules. Maybe you'd write a true story about the everyday object brought from home. Maybe you'd write a poem, something along the lines of the William Stafford piece we'd just shared, a poem which listed the kinds of things he might write about in his journal. Maybe you'd start a story, something like the Nicholson Baker excerpt, where with unusual attention to his shoes and shoelaces he described just how he walked. Maybe the mirror, or whatever object you drew from the bag, would trigger something akin to a Proustian memory. Maybe you'd simply describe all three objects.

Mindful of my own experiences with this kind of prompt, I said maybe you'd barely write anything, and just observe, perhaps scribble a note or two.

And as almost invariably happens in the workshop setting when time is set aside like this, after initial rustling, maybe a sigh or cough, the room grew quiet, but for the sound of a group of people writing.

After we shared what we came up with, I handed

out another essay, "Take This Fish and Look at It," which I'd first read in Fairbanks in the mid '80's. I loved teaching the piece then, and was happy to rediscover it as I prepared for the class. Written by nineteenth century entomologist, Samuel Scudder, the essay explains a student assignment Scudder had once been given. Asked to observe a fish, Scudder felt as if he'd seemingly exhausting the subject after ten minutes. His professor, however, instructed him to continue looking. The ten minutes stretched into a whole afternoon, then a whole evening (though the fish was at the laboratory on campus, the professor had urged Scudder to keep thinking about it), then through two more full days.

The result?

Though Scudder finally was given permission to throw away that fish — and was immediately given more fish to observe — he realized the continued close observation allowed him insights he'd never have achieved otherwise. He carried that lesson with him through the rest of his life: there would *always* be more to notice.

In a single three-hour session we could only do so much, I said to the group. But we can always get started on at least a piece or two. And afterward we can always keep at it and do so much more.

The map? As I write this, I don't have a GPS in my car. I'm not much interested in that technology, not even for my rental cars, not even when I'm driving to distant rural places, or along edgy city blocks. I don't (yet) have a phone that can call up a map and redirect me. My phone doesn't take pictures. I know: I'm stupid about these things, and stubborn. I was late to owning a computer, late to opening an email account, late to buying a cell phone. I still like my dictionary, and I like my maps.

Certainly, yes, I'm stubborn. But I'm not impossible. Increasingly, when I'm by a printer, I"ll print out a map after I look up a destination on the computer. But mainly I still rely on my road atlas to get from place to place.

Over the years, as my atlas gets pages torn, or has pages fall out, I continue to make do for as long as I can. But when I find one of those truck stop convenience stores with half-price road atlases, I'll buy a new one, and then I'm set, at least for the next while. The old one I toss in the trunk, thinking I'll make use of it someday.

Prior to my Denver workshop I'd recently moved, and discovered several of these old atlases in a box in the closet. I brought these with me, and when the time came to begin a second writing exercise—we'd already done "mirror," which included some aspect of "more"—I asked participants to write down one or two states they'd lived in at some point of their lives, and to write down one or two states they hadn't lived in but had either enjoyed visiting, or hoped to visit.

Each of us shared, and I took my old atlases, made a show of ripping the page with the named state—or half the state if it was one of those big states that stretched over two pages—and handing it over. The group could now look at their individual maps as they'd earlier looked at their individual objects, as they'd earlier looked at the mirror.

So there was something else to write about. That meant we could get started now, not in five minutes, five hours, five days, or longer. Writers are meant to write (though so many of us will seize any excuse not to).

A good writing prompt, with a little theater thrown in, can only help.

9
Talk, Talk, Talk

For so many of us, what can be more natural than talking. Talk, talk, talk. We talk with family, friends, strangers, at work, on errands, over the phone. We yell, whisper, joke, speak out of the side of our mouth. Maybe we practice ventriloquism. We can just as easily do all that talking on the page, especially the ventriloquism. After all, what do we do as writers, but allow characters to speak who cannot possibly speak for themselves.

From the first story I ever wrote, I enjoyed writing dialogue. I liked putting words in character's mouths, especially enjoyed having a character say something, another character offer a quick reply, then have the initial character return with the response. I'd type more quickly then, the words shooting down the page. The hard part was always getting characters to a place where they could have a conversation worth having. But once I got them there, I liked letting them talk, and had a knack for it.

But what does that mean, a knack for writing dialogue?

And what does it mean if you feel you don't have that knack? Does it mean you're uncomfortable putting words in people's mouths? Does it mean you're not very good at it?

For me, it means that as a writer, when writing dialogue, I get out of the way and let a character talk, whether in poem, story, or nonfiction. Six of those words bear repeating: I get out of the way.

In other words, my trick is to let my characters talk naturally, without authorial intrusion, or editorializing. Sometimes it means a throwaway word or two, like "yeah," or "I know," just like in real life. Sometimes it means much more. If the conversation is going somewhere, so much the better. But even if the conversation is going nowhere, we're still writing, and engaging in writing practice, and if the conversation is going nowhere, well, that, too, reveals something about the characters, perhaps that they're avoiding something, or that they're shallow. And, if we decide to keep going on the piece, it's up to us, the writers, to pay attention, and somehow make something special of the avoidance, or the shallowness.

And speaking of talk, especially with dialogue, one of the best and most obvious writing tips is to not just reread what we've written, but to reread what we've written by reading it aloud. That way our ear can catch what sounds wrong. And that works especially well for dialogue.

For some writers that's the best single piece of advice they can ever put into practice. In fact, some writers take it even further, composing first drafts by talking into a recording device. At some point, they'll transfer the spoken words onto a computer screen, or if theirs is a certain sensibility, onto paper.

If writing were talking, we'd all be writers most all the time. But I'm afraid it just doesn't work that way. I can understand those writers who don't write, who think of themselves as writers, who incessantly talk about writing, and then not produce. I understand because in theory they'd like to write, and more than anything they really want to have a whole body of work to point to, or at least a book, or at least one fully realized poem, story, or essay. Then they'd have something to really talk about.

Once, these talkers must have encountered writing

that inspired them, as all writers have. Likely, they're still reading work that inspires. And likely they've written something at some time that showed real talent, real promise. They might even have exquisite taste and a special love of words. But what they've never fully realized is that all writers have been similarly inspired, and all writers have talent and tastes. All of us love words, and we're all struggling in our own ways. But what makes us writers is we've been writing, are writing, and will continue writing, and it's the creation of that new work that makes writers writers. I'll say it as simply as possible: writers write.

Writers write because they have the faith, desire, or need to sit and write in lieu of other activities, especially when there's no guarantee of reward. Publication, or, god forbid, money, can take years and almost certainly will not be commensurate with the effort.

Once I attended a writers' symposium in the community I lived. According to the dictionary, symposium means a convivial party (as after a banquet in ancient Greece) with music and conversation, a social gathering at which there is free interchange of ideas. A symposium can also mean a more formal meeting.

I attended a symposium, all right, and the several days of nonstop talking about writing drove me crazy. I learned that many of the attendees were attending because they didn't yet write, but wanted to, and had extraordinary life experiences. I wondered why, with so many hopeful and intelligent people gathered who wanted to write, and so many practicing published writers present, there wasn't a structure inside the symposium to offer participants tools to actually do just that. But, alas, it was just a symposium, and the organizers just wanted everybody to talk.

If I were impatient then, I'm more so now. If we're going to talk about our writing, at some point we'd be better served to have new writing to talk about. We've got to shut up, sit down, and do it.

But I'm usually too polite. So I've learned to keep proper distance from the full-time talkers. And when I'm running a class and find myself with a talker who's threatening to hijack the class, that's okay. It's my class, and I'm the one with the leash, which isn't very long. We can talk later, I'll say gently, or more forcefully if warranted.

For now, we're going to write, I might say, and then write some more.

During the session, the talk will be in service to the writing.

When talk transcends talk, then we're getting somewhere. Write it down, I might say. Write down your every word. Stop talking, and write it as a story. Or stop talking, and write it as a scene of a play. Don't stop writing. And then when you're done, read it aloud. How does it sound? If you've taken a wrong turn, and lost the thread, you'll hear it. If you've written a wrong word or phrase, it'll sound false, and you'll hear it. Write something wrong? That's okay. All you have to do is change it. No need keeping it and diminishing the rest.

And if you can't tell the difference between what sounds good and bad, that's okay too. You just need to find a teacher who can guide you to read more closely, write more stories, create more scenes, take more classes, meet fellow writers, find more teachers.

I've never written a traditional play (my two theater pieces, *Portrait of an Artist as Santa Claus* and *Trump Sonnets or: How I've Taken on Donald Trump (and Won)* are both offshoots of my readings, and are not traditional plays), but ought to. I won't say it would be easy, but I know how I could get started. I'd go back and create a new list of names from A-Z, or else take a shortcut, anything to come up with a character. I'd give the character a friend. Or an enemy. Or a mother, father, sibling, child. It doesn't matter what, since we're just getting started.

I could ask about the hands, hair, teeth, and everything else, but probably wouldn't. More likely, I'd ask what was the first thing that person said today, and to whom. I could ask about that person's voice. High? Low? An accent? What else might distinguish it? What does that person say when he or she gets angry. And when was the last time that happened, and what triggered the emotion?

And, of course, I could go on and on, asking questions, and answering them. Just like there are only so many stories, and the rest are variations, so it is with writing exercises.

For this one, I'd realize one character in that way, and then another. Maybe they'd already be in the same place. If not, I'd figure a way to get them there. They'd talk. And, if necessary, there would be a third character. And a fourth.

Or I could just recreate Sylvia and Alfred.

The hardest part is always making the time to get started writing.

The next hardest part is making the time to continue after a promising start.

The next hardest part is making the time to properly finish.

It's always okay to fail. It's all part of the practice.

10
Read, Read, Read

When I taught semester-long Creative Writing classes, at some point midway through the term I'd bring in two or three dozen poetry collections from my personal library, another dozen or two literary journals, and slide them to the middle of the table. Your assignment for the next half hour, I said, is to pick up one or two, or more, and then do with it as you will. It might mean initially choosing a book because it's by a particular author. Or maybe choosing one because of the cover, or title. It might mean then taking a book or journal, and reading the first poem, then the second, then the third. It might mean reading that first poem, then rereading it twice more before continuing. It might mean beginning with the last poem, then going to the one preceding. It might mean randomly opening a page and reading a poem, or leafing through the book in a more calculated manner before stopping. It might mean studying the table of contents before opening to a specific title.

Or it might mean barely going into the book at all, taking the title, or a particular poem title, as a trigger to start writing poetry or prose, maybe writing something with an identical title, or using the title as the first line or sentence of something wholly new.

In that way, this exercise with the books, was similar to the exercise with the hats and shoes, or with the mirror and the map. Or with the postcards. But since these were books that were before us, objects that we ourselves potentially aspired to be creating, there was an extra element to the exercise.

The 1993-1994 year in Seattle when I was writing so much poetry as I convalesced from my illness, every month I'd take the bus to the big downtown public library. I knew just where to go in the stacks, so didn't stay long, just enough to browse the contemporary poetry section and pick out thirty or forty slim books. I could tell by writer, or publisher, or back cover blurb, if a book would do. I'd carry them like that to the checkout, and they'd easily fit in my pack. I'd open one or two on the bus ride back, then would keep them by my bedside to dip into at my leisure. From some books I might sample one or two poems which disappointed me, then leafed through the rest, confident I could stick the volume, and the author, at the bottom of the pile. From others I might read several poems at a sitting, and then return to read more over the next weeks. If I found delight in even a single poem from a single collection, I'd consider the library run a success. Of course, with thirty or forty books to sample, every month I found poems to enjoy and learn from.

The method was almost identical to what I'd done a few years before when I was out of graduate school, and engaged in my poetry self-study. Already I was much further along than the first times I went into the poetry stacks in Fairbanks. Then, I was more comfortable sampling contemporary fiction, which I knew something about, or composition or Creative Writing pedagogy, which I was so interested in, or even literary criticism, which made sense since it helped me with my papers for literature classes.

But contemporary poetry?

All I recognized in the stacks were the writers who had written poems Professor B or Professor E used in handouts, or referred to in a class. Lowell, Bishop, Frost: those were names I knew, even if I didn't yet know the work. There were other names, so many names, including writers I first heard about from my fellow students. I remember two or three had mentioned a poet, Sharon Olds. One evening in the stacks, I came upon her first collection, *Satan Says*, and opened to the title poem.

I couldn't believe what I'd read, only I'd never read anything quite like it, loved it, so had found another writer I could follow, another piece of work to model my own after.

That year in Seattle, when I found a writer I particularly liked, I did what what I'd always done, and read as much as I could by the writer, finding additional collections, whether on my next library run, or at a bookstore.

Reading poems I admired always inspired the next round of my own. I might decide to consciously write a poem in the voice of a particular writer, or a poem in my own voice, but take some aspect of that writer's work—setting, subject matter, language—to propel me. At one point I even wrote a series of poems about some of these writers.

I'd talk about this with my students, encouraging them to try similar experiments with the poems from the books they'd gathered from the table and taken home.

When I do single-session workshops, I'm less apt to spread all those poetry collections on the table and instruct the class to browse, though I might. It's just not something I want to rush through, and that exercise needs time. I'm more likely to show off books like Natalie Goldberg's *Writing Down the Bones*, anthologies of writer interviews, recent copies of *Poets & Writers* magazines, perhaps a few journals, and explain various resources, including those found on-line. Recently, though, I went through an old box and found two dozen copies of the *Lilliput Review*, a journal I used to subscribe to. Twelve pages an issue, measuring approximately three inches by four inches, it was small, all right, as befitting its name. Poems were less than ten lines, and many were half that length or shorter, so two or three poems might comfortably fit on a single miniature page. The best of the work was ingenious. Since the journal itself was so modest, when I've shared this with writing workshops, I could get my point across quickly. And there was even an additional lesson: anyone could publish in virtually any format.

When I visit schools, except for the largest groups, my program is interactive. With fifth-graders and older, if the day's schedule allows, I'll strive to make time for a question-and-answer session, though won't without first doing a show-and-tell of my books and CDs, which helps explain my background as a writer, musician, and Alaskan. I've asked students to bring paper and pen to all of our meetings—after all, we're writers here!—so when the time comes for questions, I ask them to *write* the questions—and will usually ask them to write down at least three, while I play what I call music-to-write-questions-by on my fiddle, so they can ask about my writing and books, my music and CDs, and Alaska.

Occasionally, I'm asked what advice I'd give to anyone wanting to write.

That's easy, I tell students. You've got to be a reader. When I was your age, I read books. At some point I realized all these writers had stories to tell—and I could tell my stories too.

There were so many good books out there that you could never read too much.

In another setting, I might explain how I've read many of the classics—and though I was not an English major as an undergraduate, I took two literature courses back then, and then took several more in graduate school. And as an MFA candidate in fiction writing, I completed a reading list that included Chaucer, Dickens, Eliot, Flaubert, Twain, Conrad, Joyce, Chekhov, Faulkner, and so many of the others, and passed a comprehensive exam. Reading those books taught me there were many ways to effectively tell a story.

I'm not a scholar, but I've read plenty of fiction and poetry, thought about it, and wrote about it in graduate school. Anyone who thinks they can be a writer without knowing other books that have been written, and the current state of the art, needs to think more deeply.

And then to read some of those books.

11
Speaking of Voices

Working as a touring artist since 1995, I've learned more than I've ever wanted about the performing arts field. One happy byproduct is that while I've long had friends who were writers and string-band musicians, I've made plenty of new friends who perform in various kinds of theater shows, or who dance, play other genres of music, or work as agents, or theater managers.

I sometimes hesitate to call what I offer "a show" since it's more accurately an anti-show, especially when solo. Having started doing this work in rural Alaska, I grew comfortable working with no props other than my words and music. Yet that was enough to hold attention even though I came from another culture. It's the content of the work—and, perhaps, my sense of staying present in the moment—that has kept me going all these years without elaborate technical requirements, or special lighting. I just act like myself: a fiddler, writer, and storytelling Alaskan. I'll sometimes joke that if a real actor came along to do my same solo performance, someone who could recite my poems, play fiddle tunes, tell the kinds of stories I tell, he'd likely be a lot more successful than me, the original guy who's still going around doing the work.

But I digress.

I mention all this because for years I've had a favorite routine on stage where sometime in the midst of the music, poetry, and stories, I ask, rhetorically, if anybody knows the real secret to becoming a writer.

If I've already talked about reading, a clever student will raise a hand and repeat that as an answer. I'll nod, and say yes, reading is important. Reading is *very important*, I'll say, repeating the line, and then add: But reading is no secret. This, I say, is a secret. A *big* secret.

There may be other answers, but I can always safely wave them off. I'm tricky, I tell them. And this secret is tricky. What I'm after is something else, a secret that calls to mind my friendship with some of the marvelous mimes and magicians I've been fortunate to meet in my travels.

Here, I say with a straight face, and just like that, all matter-of-fact, go into my pocket, and pull out a pen, which I proudly brandish.

This might elicit a few groans. I know what they're probably thinking. The tall, bearded guy on stage with the glasses and curly hair has pulled a pen out of his pocket. So what?

Who ever loses things? I ask.

A few kids raise their hand. I hate to lose things, I say, but if I do, I always have this. And so I go into my pocket, and pull out a second pen.

I wait a beat, then say that like lots of people, I sometimes lose things more than once. And so I go into my pocket and pull out a third pen.

The groans have turned into laughs.

Then I say that if I only have a few pens on me, I get nervous, so always have a few more, so then I pull out a fourth pen, a fifth, a sixth, and on and on, pulling out a dozen or more of various shapes, sizes, and colors. The laughs can get riotous.

Ken Waldman is always ready to write, I say. When he has an idea, he won't forget it. He'll always be able to write. Who here has ever forgotten an idea?

By now there's even more laughing, and most of the

kids have their hands raised. They've *all* forgotten ideas, or at least claimed to. Sometimes I'm even lucky enough to have one of the kids yell out something like this: Yeah, so what that you have a lot of pens. What are you going to write on?

If I'm that lucky, I can answer that I'm so very glad you asked.

Otherwise, I have to do the work myself, and explain that while I might have lots of pens, I better have something to write on. So I go into another pocket, make a big deal of pulling out my little notebook, which I flip through, and show pages filled with my near-illegible scrawl.

Of course, I continue, if I happen to lose *that* book, I have this one, and pull out another little notebook, which I show off to the assembly.

By then I'm often back near to the beginning, my legerdemain greeted with groans.

But they're friendly groans now. I know I've made my point, though I have one final joke, this one for the teachers. I mention how at one school my pocket full of pens so thoroughly astounded and confused a first-grade boy that he yelled out, But how do you run?

My answer then, which I repeat for the adults: Not as quickly as I used to. No, not nearly so fast.

And while the pens make good theater—anything to hold attention so I can make additional points—there's truth in my so-called magic. I usually have at least three or four pens in one of my pockets, often carry more, and always have a little notebook or two. I'm not kidding when I say that I get nervous if I don't have them on me.

During the middle stages of my illness time, I spent several months reading all manner of books about health and healing. That winter I happened onto Norman Cousins' *Anatomy of an Illness*. I took to heart his prescription of laughter as healing force. My friend I lived with for those months had a TV and a tape player for movies. Many nights we spent watching films from the public library's collection. We watched silent ones with Charlie Chaplin and Buster Keaton; early classics with The Marx Brothers, W.C. Fields, Laurel and Hardy, and Abbott and Costello; and ones featuring names I knew from my lifetime, from The Three Stooges to Lenny Bruce to Woody Allen to Robin Williams.

I watched intently, and realized that while Norman Cousins' formula worked best for him. I needed something more participatory, more dynamic. Even back then, in one of my pockets were pen and paper. After watching the movies I knew what to do. Since the worst of my physical crisis had abated, I could at least write. After viewing each movie, I thought I'd get added benefit by writing poems in the voices of the comics. The first one, for Groucho Marx, was a sonnet.

And so I'd found a form.

For the silent stars, I wrote sonnets that described scenes in which they might have appeared. For the rest, I tried to be true. Lenny Bruce was appropriately profane. Cheech and Chong, appropriately high—I titled that one "Cheech and Chong Off Drugs" and their conversation, each in character, examined how Cheech was high all right, not on drugs, but on air, which to this day allows me to share the poem in high schools, where it's one of my popular ones, and shows students that, yes, poems (and sonnets) can be about things they know about; I always smile how the three magic words *Cheech and Chong* can make an unruly high school bunch shut up and pay attention.

In middle schools I might share my Three Stooges poem, which is appropriately slapstick.

I explain that it was only by carrying pen and paper on me, by having that kind of access, that I was able to watch something, then write about it before I forgot the impulse. That was writers do. That's the secret.

And there's one more thing, I'll often add. Whenever you write something, always keep it. Don't throw it away. You never know when it will come in handy. You can always revise it, and by having a start, you've done the absolute hardest part.

In other settings I can explain how that comedy sonnet sequence—those poems written in voices—was a precursor to other projects. Months later I wrote another sonnet sequence, one inspired by writers, where if I didn't always capture their voices, I at least tried to capture some aspect of their writing and their lives. Later I wrote a sequence of sports-related sonnets.

Even later, in 2006, housesitting for a friend who owned a television, one night I watched the Daily Show, which inspired me to write a political sonnet for comedian and host, Jon Stewart. The next day I wrote a sonnet about the torture that had gone on at Abu Ghraib, which was currently in the news. Over the next weeks, on tour amidst gigs, and then preparing for a job in Alaska, I wrote several more topical poems, all sonnets, including one in the voice of George W. Bush. That was the one that really got me going. My first three weeks in Alaska that May and June, living in a cabin without electricity, I wrote two, sometimes three sonnets each day, the majority in the voice of the president.

By the end of August, Ridgeway Press published that collection. Months earlier, writing the poems, I was again back at one of my personal tricks: making a list to write about, then writing the poems until I had crossed out every last item.

And with the Donald Trump presidency, I took what I learned from writing the George W. Bush book. Three years into the presidency, I've written approximately 300 sonnets about the man and his times, enough for four full-length volumes. It's how I'm processing this historic era.

My refrain to apprentice writers: If I can do this, so can you.

12
Poetry as Headlines (and Poetry as News)

When I'm waiting in line at the grocery I'm sure I'm not the only one who can't help staring at the bold headlines from the celebrity tabloids. That's why they're at the check-out counter. As teasers, they rarely disappoint me: whether it's the latest Bill Clinton, Hillary Clinton, or Barack Obama fabulation, or a slightly more plausible (and even more provocative) Britney Spears, Angelina Jolie, or Tom Cruise one-liner.

I may not have an idea of the identities of some of these "celebrities," the season's bachelor, or bachelorette, or reality show breakthrough star. But no matter. The headlines are sensational enough to draw me in, at least for a few seconds. And there's always the chance that the latest Clinton or Obama escapade might somehow relate to my ongoing Donald Trump sonnet project.

If I have a substantial writing workshop on my calendar, I'll pick up the publication that's either gaudiest or thickest, and throw it in with my mushrooms, avocados, and garlic. Maybe the check-out cashier or my line mates will think I'm an utter idiot, wasting three dollars on such frivolity. Maybe they'll be secretly envious. After all, this isn't the everyday news—nor is it exactly what any of us will find on the Daily Show. More likely, no one cares what I'm buying or is even looking; so many of us are barely surviving our own problems.

But with the current price of old postcards, if I think about things in a writerly and teacherly way, it's a sign of the times, and a bargain: a front page with larger-than-life headlines, then another thirty-one pages that will dependably feature several more strange lines that may, or may not, approach, or trigger, poetry. Depending on the particular workshop, I've had terrific results taking out scissors, parceling the headlines in various ways. Just like with some of my other exercises, we can randomly choose our headline prompt, or I can distribute them as I see fit, or we can all write about some same twisted scenario.

To launch us forward, I might share one of my poems, "Satan Found!" which owed its existence to this prompt. Or share others of similar aesthetic.

Satan Found!

As you drove east
into Missouri, I read
headlines, skimmed
the outlandish columns,
then told you how
last October Jack Miracle
of Sulphur, Oklahoma
watched a bull moose leap
barbed wire to mate
with Esmerelda, his mare,
and how, after naming the foal
Satan, Miracle castrated it,
stating, God told me to.

I thought you'd laugh—
you know, tabloids
as bible. But no. Sober
eyes still on the road,

> you said, "Honey, I want
> your baby." The next moment
> wisps of smoke rose
> from the steering wheel—
> and the car went dead.

Some writers will naturally gravitate to quieter subjects, and quieter treatments (so might politely balk at this one). Others will revel in the outrageousness of the possibilities. My take is that it's all good, especially if in a short workshop I'm in some small way opening writers to a wider variety of poems. I'm only doing my job by pointing out that with poetry all is possible. Besides, with this one, like most of the others, we're only going to spend 15 or 20 minutes. If a single writer finds a single start that's a keeper, we're all furthered.
What do we have to lose?

Some of the most quoted lines of 20th century American poetry are these by William Carlos Williams from the long poem, "Asphodel, That Greeny Flower."

> "It is difficult
> to get the news from poems
> yet men die miserably every day
> for lack
> of what is found there."

William Carlos Williams isn't going to show up in the *National Enquirer*, nor am I suggesting we put him there (though—note to self—there's a certain appeal to somehow refer to him, or someone like him, by name in a poem triggered by one of those outrageous headlines).
Williams can sometimes be difficult—and he's right that it can often be difficult to get the news from poems—but toward the end of his life he wrote the poem which included those lines above.

Poetry as news?

We can go there, too. Early Tuesday morning, September 11, 2001, I remember waking up in the spare bedroom of the house of my Austin banjo pal, Jerry. The preceding weekend I'd attended a music conference in Kerrville, where I played a short set with Jerry and another friend, Tom. The idea was to meet people there in Kerrville who in theory would eventually hire us for gigs. It's a version of a model I've been chasing for almost as long as I've been doing this work.

At Kerrville, I also wanted to let people know about a show with Jerry on Wednesday, September 12, at the Cactus Cafe, an Austin listening room, located on the University of Texas campus. The event, sponsored by the Austin Friends of Traditional Music, had a little bit of a buzz to it, at least as I recognized such things. Jerry was from the community, and was greatly respected for his playing. Through Jerry, I'd been meeting people. It helped that for Wednesday morning, September 12, we had booked an interview, which would include playing live music, on a popular show on KUT, the big public radio station. We'd reach thousands of listeners. Since the Cactus Cafe had a modest capacity, which we heard was already half-filled with reservations, we were confident. I'd been to Austin previously, but wasn't well-known. But I'd been learning how all of this was cumulative, and was confident that my mix of traditional music and poetry at this venue, coupled with the twenty-minute radio spot, couldn't help but jump-start a network of Austin fans.

Like so many of us in so many places, the morning of September 11, 2001 I was in front a television—in this case watching the day's inexorable progression of events with Jerry's wife and daughter. Of course the radio spot the next day was quickly canceled. But the Cactus Cafe show involved other considerations. While Jerry had email, I didn't, and at that time there was no guaranteed way to get word out about a canceled show. And if we did cancel, I knew how complicated it had been to pick up the gig in the first place, and wasn't optimistic we'd get a return date.

Even at best, this one wasn't going to be about making money. And with the historic tumult of those days, this was going to be the most minor of inconveniences. But the Cactus Cafe was also a bar and was going to have people there drinking who'd like to check out whatever was on stage. The event had been well-advertised. And, really, the alternative was for Jerry and I to sit at home with his wife and daughter, and watch the continuing reports from New York City and Washington D.C. There was nothing wrong with that, but we didn't have to do it.

Late Tuesday evening, after consulting with Jerry and talking to my contacts at the Cactus Cafe and the Austin Friends of Traditional Music, we decided to play the show. At a certain point, it was an easy choice. People were going to show up and we still wanted to do it. However, in order for me to perform and be true to myself, I understood I had better write a poem to share about what had happened the previous day.

I wrote a poem on Tuesday night, and spent part of the next day typing it, formatting it, and going to a copy center to print several dozen copies on cardstock, enough so I could distribute one to whomever attended the performance.

We drew approximately twenty people—a fragment of what we'd been expecting prior to the September 11 attacks but reasonable for the circumstances—who were grateful for the music, the poetry, and the community. The next day, in the same spare room I'd been sleeping in, Jerry and I recorded a single track of me reading the September 11th poem over Jerry's banjo before I picked up the fiddle to join him on the tune. Then we burned a few dozen CDs. Within weeks the music and poem were receiving a scattering of radio airplay nationally.

It felt useful to make art out of the tragedy, though as

those strange September days unfurled, it seemed like *every* poet was trying to make sense of that terrible time. The following weeks I led a writing workshop in San Antonio, which felt necessary and powerful, and then spent two days in residence at a college in West Texas, where I felt thoroughly bardic, traveling from the cosmopolitan capital city of Austin to deliver news.

If that was it, I'd have been fine. But in this case the episode felt unfinished. How unfinished, I didn't know until October 11, sitting in a friend's kitchen in Colorado, trying to digest that week's news: the rubble still mountainous in downtown New York City, a war in Afghanistan, packets with anthrax going through the mail.

So, October 11 I wrote a companion poem to the September 11 piece. November 11, on Vancouver Island, I wrote a third poem. December 11, in Alaska, I wrote the fourth. And I continued the sequence through September 11, 2002, when I took time while in New Orleans to check in on the anniversary.

That might have been the end, but January 2013, four and a half months later I was back in Austin at Jerry's. By then I had a website, another book, another CD. Personally, I might have been on the move, but as I crisscrossed the continent and followed the news, I sensed something particularly skewed. One of the days in Austin, sitting in Jerry's living room, almost the exact spot I wrote the poem about September 11, I quickly wrote another poem, this one about what appeared to be a call to war in Iraq.

As poets and writers, our task is to respond to information clearly and honestly. Every day, the big news and small news beckon us to do just that.

Because of September 11, I wrote a poem a month for a year. Twelve poems, and then a thirteenth poem several months later. That wasn't so much.

As an engaged citizen, can you do the same?

13
Three Short Lessons, Compliments of Professor B

Professor B's best lesson was a long handout, where he laboriously broke down some of the options he was considering for one of his poems. He took the exact same words, and showed how he might experiment turning the poem into long two-line stanzas, long four-line stanzas, or long eight-line stanzas, or else breaking the lines at various spots to make the poem longer, but thinner, with much shorter two-line, four-line stanzas, and eight-line stanzas. He explored what the same words looked like in three-line or five-line stanzas. He printed out a draft with no stanza breaks at all, and then with no line breaks at all, turning it into a prose poem.

It was revelatory to see how Professor B could subtly toy with meaning as he took an already substantial poem, and attempted to improve it through emphasizing the exact placement of words. Could any of us argue with the purposeful care Professor B lavished on his poems?

The nature of good poetry had to be to make absolute best use of the language in any one poem. After taking a class with Professor B, I better understood how that was a worthy ambition, which made me wonder how poetry so often suffered from such a horrible reputation.

But then, of course, I knew.

While poetry could be absolutely wonderful, not all of it was. And some of the more celebrated contemporary poetry was written as if for an exclusive, private audience. The work not only defied any easy understanding—and that was okay since good poetry didn't have to be "easy"—but the worst examples defied logic. Why was this the work that was sometimes so celebrated? Was it the fault of the individual poets? The fault of the critics and reviewers?

Maybe that was the point—it was a big world out there, and it could always be argued that poems I viewed as willfully obscure, another reader might view as ones that more perfectly mimicked the broken-down nonsense of our world.

But if that was the point, I'd choose to read something else.

The first poem I ever got published was written in response to an exercise in Professor B's class. His prompts were more prescriptive than I'd have preferred, but that didn't mean they weren't useful. Asked to write an instruction poem that was "a lesson," I wrote "Three Lessons in Taking Off Clothes," which twenty-five years later remains a favorite for high-school and college readers unaccustomed to sexy poetry. I'm always heartened by the positive response I get to the last lines of the second stanza, which explains the end of the second lesson: Invite a friend/to take your clothes off for you.

The next years, I borrowed the instruction assignment to write a poem about learning to play fiddle, a poem about learning to play banjo, a poem about the ritual of washing dishes in a cabin without running water. I've written a number of poems about teaching writing.

One of Professor B's favorite prompts was simply to instruct us to go for a walk, and then write about it. The idea was to get outside, and report. Professor B has written his own successful sequence, taking the same walk each month to a favorite spot where he sat and observed the changing Interior Alaska seasons.

For Professor B's class assignment, I wrote one about walking to my Fairbanks mailbox, a poem which turned out to be the appropriate opener for my first collection. Three years later, in Sitka, I wrote one about walking through an overgrown Native graveyard. And later, living in Nome, a place where I spent so much time walking, that became my way to see the community, and to write about it.

14
Writer as Scavenger, Poet as Sculptor

For a few years I visited an inordinate number of friends who had purchased, or were given, magnetic poetry kits. In those houses, most every time I had reason to walk into the kitchen, I'd gravitate to the refrigerator, and peruse the words and letters on magnets. Sometimes I might delight in the few short, clever poems which had been allowed to remain intact. Other times I might find neat columns of words awaiting me, or a temptation of single words stuck randomly across the refrigerator surface.

I usually lingered at the refrigerator to try my hand at it. Magnetic poetry certainly appealed to my sensibilities. There was the sense of play, the tactile pleasure of lifting the little rectangular magnets and setting them next to one another to invent a strange little poem or epigram I'd otherwise have never thought of. These ready-to-go words coupled with the constraints of the form — after all, we were limited to the words and letters on the magnets — lent a quasi-formal quality to the exercise.

I came up with a few surprisingly good ones, but never followed my own advice of copying them. In that way they were like some of the occasional poems I wrote on school whiteboards. Once they were erased, they were gone. But that was okay. These were modest poems written for practice, and there were always more where they came from.

Some day, when I have the time and inclination, it's on my list to make my own non-magnetic poetry kit, a thousand words on cardstock, plus dozens of suffixes, prefixes, and punctuation marks. Then I'd give a few hundred of these to workshop attendees and see what they come up with. When the words are already there, it really is somehow easier.

Everyone can find a process that works for them. Though I don't keep a journal, I recommend it for others, since that might be the routine that best helps a particular writer. In lieu of journals, what I've kept—or tried to keep—are early drafts of incomplete work, which might be from recent writing workshops, but range all the way back to graduate school, and work I did in workshops then, or when writing along with students in composition classes. Some of the notebooks I've successfully lugged for more than thirty years now. Some, despite my best efforts, seemed to have disappeared into the void, undoubtedly beside the rest of my lost past.

I've always intended to get back to those old pieces, most of them prose. When I do finally clear away the time and space, I'll treat them in various ways. One will be a technique I first used to write a successful poem in a way I'd never before quite imagined.

A casual friend from my time in Nome, Jim Lawhon, wrote me the summer after he climbed Denali, the Alaska mountain that's the highest on the continent. I don't remember whether he made the summit—I believe he did—only that his letter was not a letter in any regular sense. He'd sent me a handwritten journal entry about the ascent, without further explanation.

Frankly, I didn't know how to respond, so didn't write him back, and instead kept his paper amid a pile of other sheets. Periodically, looking for something else, I'd find Jim's letter, reread it, and then furrow my brow. I wanted to throw it out, since I already had enough papers cluttering my days. But that felt wrong. Clearly, there was something I was supposed to do. But what?

And one day I knew, or thought I did, and in retrospect the answer was obvious. Jim knew I wrote poems. If I were to take his journal entry and somehow make it into poetry, I could send him what I'd written, and be finished with it. Why he didn't tell me this directly, I don't know. But that had to have been the point.

And if it wasn't, well, that was too bad.

The resulting poem? That was where the sculpting came in. The original journal entry was a full page of small print, maybe 500 words. I combed through it again and again, and thought if I just pared most everything away, maybe I'd have something.

15,000 Feet, Denali
for Jim Lawhon

Blue ice
chips and skitters.

Three breaths. Step.
Right foot. The ax.

His pack
would have him backwards,

tumbling. He trembles,
feels sweat trickle

and clump in his beard.
Above, God's porch,

his summons.
Climb, he hears.

So he kicks.
Foot in. The ax.

Because of the brevity—this whole poem was less than 50 words—it made sense to ultimately choose two-line stanzas, which gave the words room to breathe.

Better, by having successfully finished this, I could send it to Jim, which I put in the mail along with his original journal entry (which I now wish I'd kept, so I could show all that I cut).

It's easy to see that any journal entry could be treated similarly. And if there's enough time and space from the original writing, it hardly feels like yours, which makes it easier to be fully objective, so as to be properly ruthless with the cuts. As is, I've been doing this long enough that not only can I not remember the impulse behind some of my published work, I can't even remember having once done the writing.

Recently, visiting a college Creative Writing class, I was asked to respond to a student's prose poem that badly needed tightening. I took it home, spent proper time, and suggested changes that saved the language, but shortened an already brief poem by half.

Sure, what I offered was only editing. But when half or three quarters of the words are eliminated, it feels more like sculpting. When doing so reveals the power inside a piece of writing, it may even go beyond sculpting to alchemy.

15
One Minute (Life or Death)

When I taught freshman composition and developmental writing in Fairbanks, I thought my first assignment was a good, ungraded warm-up: take an activity, any activity, and describe one minute of doing it. Depending on choice of subject, that might mean describing one minute of making a sandwich, or changing the oil in a car, or skiing, or walking a dog, or, well, it could be anything.

And that was the point. Students were free to write about virtually anything. The poorer writers struggled to write a single paragraph and whined for more guidance. The better ones understood that to truly describe anything meant paying attention to detail, as explained in class and in a handout, and following through by writing those details.

The assignment, combined with an early-in-the-semester conference, meant I had a sense of the student-writer, so could more confidently nudge him or her in directions more apt to help the writing.

My second semester of teaching I was pleased to get a paper titled "One Minute of Rock Climbing," written by an older student returning to school after a divorce and career change. This student had never considered himself a writer, but had listened to what I'd said during the first class, and had wholeheartedly approached that first non-graded paper. The writing wasn't perfect, but it was good. Since it was handwritten, which was allowed for the first non-graded piece, my response was to ask him to type it, then to research climbing magazines, and send it to one for publication. With proof of submission, the student would receive an A for his first graded paper, which he could now skip.

Just as I was pleased by the paper, the student was pleased by my response. He'd made some mistakes in his past, he told me, and just wanted to restart his life with a return to school. It hadn't been easy to write this paper, he said, but it hadn't been that hard either. However, what he thought would have taken an hour to write, had taken him most of the weekend. In addition to the strong sentence-by-sentence writing, what made the essay stand out was the subject. His minute of rock climbing—which was really several minutes—focused on his thoughts when spotting for a friend who was having difficulty making a next move up a mountain. As the spotter, the writer could only watch as his friend struggled to hold on to make a next move—there was a very real chance of his friend falling, and dying. The episode had brought to mind for the writer the risks that climbers take, and the risks that all humans take.

The writer ended the piece by describing how his friend fortunately found a handhold, and pulled himself up. Then, when it was the writer's turn to climb that same stretch of rock, he managed to clamber up easily, not because he was better or stronger, but because that was the nature of the sport.

The rest of the semester the student continued to write superior papers, and some weeks later reported that a climbing magazine had indeed accepted his essay, and was going to pay him $50.

When I do my show-and-tell for high school and college students, I quickly show my eleven poetry collections, my memoir, my children's book, and my nine CDs. Then I slow down, and take out my chapbooks, that is my books which are stapled pamphlets. I have twenty-six of them, and I show them all, explaining that I've put them together thematically, and am showing them because just as I've written about things that have interested me, so can they.

The first chapbook I ever wrote included only poems set in Nome and the Bering Straits region. Other chapbooks included poems set in other parts of Alaska, poems about music, poems of relationship, comedy poems, political poems, sports poems, poems about writing, and there were more: poems about food, poems about school, poems about writing, poems about my parents, poems that were sonnets. Eight of the chapbooks were published in 1995. Eight more in 1996. The last ten in 1999. The first of the 1996 chapbooks consisted of poems about my March 2 plane crash of that year.

My student writer wrote about a rock climbing drama. I've written in depth about my plane crash. When I show that book in front of a large group of students, I ask if anyone else in the room has been in a plane crash. Usually that will get me a few nervous laughs. I continue and explain that if I were with a group this large in Alaska, chances were that we'd have had a hand or two raised in response since so many people have to fly to get places, and accidents happen. I then ask if anybody in the room has been in a car crash. Invariably, I'll see hands go up.

How about a big bike wreck, I'll ask, and more hands are raised.

If we're near mountains, I'll ask if anybody has had a big snowboard wreck or ski wreck.

Who's fallen out of a tree, I'll ask next.

Who's had broken bones?

Who's been to an emergency room?

Is there anybody else that, like me, has had a near death experience?

By then the room is often buzzing. Then I'll ask who here has written about those experiences. And that will quiet them. Only a few hands will go up, if even that many. I'll go on to say that just like I had my plane crash to write about, and one of my students had a rock climbing adventure, everybody here in this room has their own story to write.

During the question-and-answer, if there are questions about my plane crash, as there sometimes are, I'll answer by reading one or two of my poems. I hope that by showing such close description, I don't have to spell out that, yes, when you write, you want to go into such detail.

But if I have to spell it out, I'll do just that.

I self-published all twenty-six of my chapbooks. I wouldn't necessarily recommend the model for others, but I had my reasons.

Having written so many poems in the early 1990's, especially in the midst of my illness time, I was creating a body of work. Having had so many poems accepted for publication, I was confident the work had merit. Since so many of the poems fit so easily with one another inside clear categories of subject or setting, I knew I had books. Because I'd gotten so sick, I'd more deeply understood my own mortality. There were not going to be any guarantees. Not now. Not in the future. But I did have all these completed poems, and I was impatient, especially after my first queries and contest entries failed.

Though chapbooks have existed in some form for over three centuries, they're currently most in vogue with contemporary poetry, though I think we'll see more fiction and creative nonfiction chapbooks in the coming years. Why not? Chapbooks can come in all sizes and shapes. They can be manufactured quickly on a budget and put together by anyone with a cheap printer and decent stapler—yet can also be hand-stitched, letterpress works of art. And while more writers now consider chapbooks not only a respectable stepping stone to a full-length poetry collection, but also a worthy end destination for a special sequence of poems that won't fit as snugly, or happily, in a full-length volume, there will always be a stigma.

I remember a writer and editor who saw my display of 26 chapbooks, two CDs, a full-length book of poetry, and called out with visible annoyance, And what have we here? A writer of chapbooks?

I didn't know this man personally, only by reputation, so the disdain was characteristic. When I pointed to my full-length collection, and mentioned by name the publisher, the editor only sniffed and said, Are you not a writer of chapbooks? Do I not see a table of chapbooks?

I shook my head, not knowing what to say. Now, if I could go back, I'd have found the chapbook titled, *Writing Lessons*, and the one titled, *Crash Stories: Plane Wreck Poems*, and given him copies.

Even more satisfying would have been to write a poem about him.

But failing that, at least I now have this short sketch, where more than a decade later I've said in so many words: Why did you have to act like such a jerk? Were you really that threatened by me? And, now, are you still so insecure?

That's one of the benefits of this work: a writer can go into the depths, poke around, and come back with insights. It's all part of the practice.

16
Places, Imaginary and Not

Staring at a map until a town, lake, river, or city opens its story is one way to pay attention to place and begin writing. Relying on a deep personal knowledge is another. Going for a walk, or a ride, is one more. Or we can start a new piece by making the place a character, bringing it to life just as we earlier brought a newly-invented character to life.

I might point to someone sitting across from me at the table and suddenly ask for a place that starts with J.

Maybe I'll hear Jackson, or Juneau, or Jupiter.

I can ask for something that starts with O.

Ohio, Oregon, Opelousas.

An I?

Ireland, Iceland, Indiana.

Here, we may not be going straight from top to bottom, but in a few minutes we're once again making an A-Z list, though I don't have to be prescriptive, of course. But I do want to get us all thinking: Asheville, Boise, California, Denmark, Eagle River, France, Graceland, Hawaii, Iceland, Jackson, Kentucky, Las Vegas, Manhattan, New Zealand, Oregon, Philadelphia, Quincy, Reno, South Dakota, Texas, Utah, Virginia, Washington, Xenia, Yellow Springs, Zanesville.

Maybe we'll choose a place we've been; maybe one we've wanted to visit; maybe one we've never much thought of. When we write, we can play it straight, or invent a spot that's totally imaginary. But now that we have a list of places, we have a way in.

Maybe the list alone is sufficient to start writing. But here are ten questions I might ask (with a few extras):

One: What color most quickly comes to mind? (why?)

Two: What season is its favorite?

Three: If the place could choose a human—anybody in history—to represent it, who would that be?

Four: What does this place most like to eat?

Five: If the place were to play a music instrument, which one would it be? (And what kind of music?)

Six: What creature is the place afraid of?

Seven: What does this place prefer: Hot or cold? Dark or light? Wet or dry?

Eight: If the place could talk, what would be its first thirteen words?

Nine: What kind of party would this place host?

Ten: If the place were to move, where would it go?

Boise Talking

We love our corn,
big stalks of summer,

football near. We love
our Blue Thunder

Marching Band,
the drums, our big-play

offense, our strong
and sturdy boys.

Let me tell you
what it means

to live in the green
of the lit, dry

city of trees.
It's our Hollywood.

Americana Boulevard,
where a young man

grows up dreaming,
perhaps to become

lineman, linebacker,
perhaps William Tell

looking at green ash
and sunset maple,

the brown hills
over and over,

loving our corn
over and over,

our prettiest girls
leading the cheers.

    While a place can be a river, city, or state, it also can be a bedroom, kitchen, bathtub, backyard, patio, street, or school. A place can be a basketball court, tennis court, swimming pool, golf course, laundromat, or bar. A place can be the interior of a car or van. A place can be the inside of your brain. A place can be a Creative Writing classroom.
    Since good teachers can teach most anything, even when they're not experts, and bad teachers can make a mess of it even when world-class talents, if you have a choice, who would you voluntarily choose to study with?
    Really, It's no different than any other decision.

How did you get to Fairbanks, people will often ask.

And often I'll answer glibly, echoing what I'd explained earlier here. When living in Seattle I'd somehow written a story which was better than anything I'd previously written. Afterward, I was confident that if I set up my life in certain ways, I could write more stories, because, having written that one story, I was now "a writer."

And while that explains how I got to Fairbanks, it doesn't explain it all.

It doesn't explain growing up, privileged, in suburban Philadelphia, with parents who quietly despised one another. For solace, I took refuge in sports and books. I excelled in tennis, and in the classroom, where I graduated near the top of my high school class, taking several advanced placement courses. At home, I was careful to be perfectly silent, anything to keep the days of fragile equilibrium going.

It doesn't explain going to college at Duke University, a school I'd chosen since it was an eight-hour drive, the furthest I could imagine, and was also south, where it was warmer. Presumably I'd play collegiate tennis, and did until I hurt my knee playing pick-up basketball. The next year I was healed, but if I'd understood at the beginning that the team had one player on full scholarship, four others on half scholarships, a roster filled with a half-dozen walk-ons, like me, who were as good as those half-scholarship players, I'd have gone elsewhere.

I thought I was going to be a Math major, since my favorite high school teacher taught Math, and I thought I had an aptitude. First semester, I got an A on material I already knew. Next semester, taking the next course in the sequence, struggling to get a C, intuitively understanding this was no longer about numbers, and I didn't have the knack to take on that kind of theoretical work, I switched my major to Management Science, which felt like applied math. Because I was already several credits ahead from my high school advanced placement courses,

I'd accidentally wandered onto the easiest path through Duke.

My remaining three years, I received mostly B's in my major, and took electives as I wished. I got a C in a Shakespeare class, a B in a contemporary fiction class, where I remember nothing of the reading list, save Thomas Pynchon's *V*, which I didn't understand (and which I reread fifteen years later after studying Pynchon in graduate school). Most of the material was as dark as I felt. I took two drawing classes, where the instructor sighed tiredly every time she glanced at my inept renderings. I also took a pair of Creative Writing workshops. The only piece I finished was about a head-case of a slumping high school tennis player who allowed his best friend to hypnotize him into getting his game back. The trick worked, at least temporarily, so the young man wanted more of it, soon learning self-hypnosis from this friend. Not surprisingly, the hypnotism soon took over his life.

Though the short story hadn't been easy to write, it had been well-received in the workshop by my fellow students, including by the one obviously talented writer there. What I'd never told anybody was how autobiographical the story was, even down to the hypnosis and self-hypnosis, and how to finish writing it I had to put myself into a trance one afternoon and force myself to sit at the typewriter.

Otherwise, I was thoroughly stuck, and it was obviously not just with the writing. My parents had their own issues so could hardly guide me, splitting up bitterly my sophomore year. And while there was a hugely respected writer in residence on campus, Reynolds Price, who by all accounts was also a wonderful and generous teacher, I didn't have a clue. Mainly, I still wished I'd have gone somewhere I could have played collegiate tennis.

After graduating, I took to the road, spent most of the year driving around, reading, drinking coffee and beer. The following winter in Boston, living with a girlfriend, I took a pair of workshops. By bringing in that same hypnotism story, which I'd been tinkering with, I established that I at least appeared like a serious writer. I wrote a couple of short new pieces, including a well-received piece about a surreal, nonsensical conversation between a man and woman on a first date. It was only a few pages long, had taken weeks to write, and it didn't seem to me to be that good.

My "day job" was the 11-7 shift at a 7-Eleven off Beacon Hill. My life might have seemed romantic. It wasn't. I was drinking lots of coffee, lots of beer. My girlfriend, who was grieving her mother who had committed suicide in the early fall, was more apt to smoke pot, and I'd sometimes join her. My girlfriend and I were the same age, and we loved each other, but that wasn't going to be enough. One night we were going to see a Grateful Dead concert and invited a friend over for dinner. We got high and the friend gave us some speed.

At the concert, my girlfriend and I started hallucinating near simultaneously, freaking us both out. We left the show, stumbling back to the apartment, where we pondered a trip to the emergency room, and wondered if we could just hold on. We weren't sure what to do, and didn't remember calling so many friends, who all rushed over. When the doorbell rang with the first of our visitors, my girlfriend opened the door wearing only a blouse.

I heard afterward we hosted quite a strange gathering that night, our Boston friends babysitting us until our fear subsided. At one point, one friend, also a Grateful Dead enthusiast, asked if our ticket stubs were in a pocket somewhere. The show might still be going on, he mused, and it would be fun to catch some of it.

The following week, coming down from the drug, I tiredly wrote a short story about a university teacher who had undergone a transformation, shedding wife, job, girlfriend, becoming a dangerously popular cult-figure poet.

It was the last piece I'd write and finish for more than five years. The Cambridge workshop thought it was quite fine. The next months I sent it to both *Playboy* and *Pent-*

house, where the fiction editor at the latter rejected it with a scrawled request to send something else. The next year in North Carolina, I actually applied to the MFA program at University of British Columbia, where I was wait-listed, and several months later learned that I'd been accepted at the last minute, but had not received the message on the telephone answering machine.

When my girlfriend went into the Peace Corps, I attempted to start a story about my time working the 11-7 shift at the Boston 7-Eleven, an upside-down time, and a writer who wasn't writing. Mirroring the sad protagonist, I couldn't write it.

I drove to Durham, North Carolina, my old college town, intending to spend a night or two. The next four and a half years, this time bouncing between Durham and Chapel Hill, were the college education I never quite received. The bookstore job was a boon. So were my days working in restaurants, where I made new friends, learned different ways of being. I saw a counselor. I bought a fiddle and started learning. I healed. The Delmore Schwartz story I read, where a young man goes into a movie theater, watches horrified as the big screen shows his father courting his mother, captured my imagination. I got the idea to write a somewhat similar story. In mine, a young man in an auction hall would be bidding against his parents.

Maybe I didn't have to leave North Carolina in order to write, but late summer 1984 that's what I did. 28 years old, I thought I should be writing, but wasn't sure I would if I stayed in North Carolina. My life was comfortable. I'd been teaching tennis again, and was making a name for myself locally as an instructor. I'd even recently played in several tournaments. I wasn't much of a fiddler yet, but I'd gotten over the very worst part, and it looked like I'd continue. I'd saved more than seven thousand dollars from teaching tennis and waiting tables.

When I reached Seattle that October, I found an apartment, and immediately began work on the story I'd been imagining, "The Auction." It took a month to complete the 15-page draft, and writing it brought to mind the struggle of writing that hypnotism story back at Duke. Though pleased to finish, I had to admit to myself that I was not much of a writer. It wasn't that the story was awful, but that it lacked something essential.

The next weeks I made a home in Seattle. I took swing dance classes, and lugged my fiddle to parties. I wasn't very good on the instrument, but was meeting musicians at every level, from the best in the region (and country) to ones starting out like me. I was dating women. I'd met Scott, who was beginning work on a novel.

But my money was dwindling. I made contacts to begin teaching tennis again, and applied for several restaurant jobs. I also paid a deposit to reserve a place in an advertising copywriting class that would begin in the spring. After a round of rejections at Seattle ad agencies, I had one manager tell me that if I took that class, I had the talent to likely land an entry level position within several months. Happy in Seattle, I recognized I needed to find work to stay there.

Early January at a square dance I met a woman, the kind of woman I thought I'd always meet, but never had. When we talked, it seemed the feeling was mutual. When we walked out together at the end of the night, I wanted to hold that feeling close, like I wanted to hold her. We went out a few nights later, and the spark felt momentous. I was already dreaming of her. I may have thought I'd found my home in Seattle. As for this woman, I didn't have to think; I knew.

She had arrived in Seattle about the same time I had, and while I wanted to write, she wanted to do visual art. We went out two more times before she told me she'd recently left a long-term relationship, and that we needed to take this slowly, and she needed time.

But I couldn't do that, at least not easily. I still didn't have a job, had no way to process this relationship but to obsess. Walking by a coffeehouse in my Capitol Hill neighborhood, I saw from an index card on a bulletin board that a writers' group was forming. I copied the phone number and called that evening. A woman answered, and I asked about the writers' group. It was her and one guy for sure, she said, and there were several others who might come. They were meeting the next night in her apartment, and hoped to meet every week, depending on who showed up and their schedules She asked about my background. When I answered, she said she hoped I could make it.

The next night I walked to her apartment. We waited, but after fifteen minutes it looked like there were just going to be the three of us: she, the other guy, and myself. There were four or five others who said they might come, she said, and laughed nervously.

It wasn't much of a meeting, only that we decided to meet again the following week, when she knew at least a few others would definitely come.

Then the guy said we should write something for next week.

Sure, I nodded.

Good idea, the woman said. Any thoughts?

The guy shook his head.

I know, I said. How about the first day in a new place. The idea had just popped into my head, but I liked it.

The woman smiled. I can do that, she said.

Me too, the guy said.

I guess I will too, I said.

The next day I started writing about a couple I'd stayed with some months earlier near Bellingham, immediately before arriving in Seattle. The husband was the brother of a medical school friend in North Carolina. There was something about his wife that seemed to encapsulate the Pacific Northwest, a place I'd never before been. The visit hadn't seemed all that momentous at the time, but I hadn't forgotten.

The couple had a gardening business, which was just

beginning to prosper. The weeks were long, and they told me how they like to worked hard and then fully relax. I arrived in time for fish tacos on Saturday evening before a long soak in their hot tub.

The next day, the wife took the afternoon off to take me mushroom picking and she brought their llama along. Returning to their house, we identified mushrooms, cooked up some of the chanterelles, along with some salmon. We drank Mexican beer. It had been a beautiful October night, too, and the hot tub afterward felt decadent.

The story, which I called, "Mushrooms," was everything "The Auction" wasn't. It was easy, it flowed, and it was fully mine, a fictional treatment of my 36 hours with this couple. It ended with the first-person narrator taking off, driving south on I-5, arriving in Seattle, where after the earlier visit north of the city, he's ready for whatever this new place will bring.

Writing the story, I felt as if I had found my voice.

The next week, I visited the writing group a second and last time, before driving to Southern California to visit a college friend. Alas, the space and time away from the Seattle woman I so wanted to be with ultimately didn't help, and it ended badly. But I had the new story, and the insight that I could write more.

The following weeks in Seattle I saw a therapist, who was helpful. At one point, when I mentioned an idea I'd had of applying to graduate school in Creative Writing in Fairbanks, and asked if I was crazy, the therapist replied that as far as graduate school in Alaska, I could apply to the program and take it from there. I might get in, or I might not. If I was admitted, I could decide to go, or not go. But as for being crazy? She smiled. That was an entirely different thing, she said, and we could talk about it.

The next week, I decided to apply to graduate school. That same week, when I was also supposed to begin the advertising copywriting class, I received a phone call from a new downtown restaurant. Three months earlier I'd dropped off a resume. Now they had finally gotten around to filling positions. From the phone conversation, I understood the meeting was a formality. The restaurant was about to open and they needed staff. The only problem was the interview would conflict with the copywriting class.

I walked downtown, met with the restaurant manager, was hired, and started training immediately. It hadn't taken much to drop the idea of writing advertising in Seattle. The next weeks I fell into a new routine, working several shifts at the restaurant, teaching tennis through a nearby parks department, continuing with the fiddle, even at last completing the story set in the Boston 7-Eleven, the one about the writer who didn't write. In May I received word that I'd been accepted in the Fairbanks program. I called the therapist I'd seen back in March to let her know the outcome of the application process, and to admit that by then it didn't feel the least bit crazy to decide to move to Alaska.

I left Seattle by ferry the last day of July, a blue moon Friday. It would take four full days by boat and van to reach Fairbanks. I had more than three weeks before my first campus responsibilities, enough time to settle in before school began, even to take a pair of trips in the Alaska Interior. Prior to the move, I may not have known anybody where I was heading, but I'd just gone through the same routine in Seattle. And over the early part of the summer I'd talked to a number of my new friends who knew people in and around Fairbanks.

So I had already heard about Professor A, and his desultory ways. But that was okay. I would give him a chance. It was a big world, and we were all doing what we could.

I'd arrive in Alaska knowing that with any luck at all, I would find my way.

And that's the real story how I got to Fairbanks.

17
Holiday and Family

Meanwhile, back in the North Carolina Piedmont more than thirty years ago, before I found my way to the bookstore, the fiddle, and all the rest, I spent almost a full year absolutely floundering. It wasn't for lack of trying. I sought healers for my body, which was breaking. I worked a series of temp jobs. For two months I interned at a small local magazine, *The Sun*.

The Sun was struggling then too, though in the next few years would become a success story for small press journals and magazines. The foundation was already there. Instead of publishing quarterly or biannually, like most publications of near-similar size and content, *The Sun* came out monthly. That meant that while the small staff may have been challenged putting each issue together, with each issue came momentum. Instead of depending on ad revenue, the magazine depended on subscribers willing to pay for a smart, eclectic mix of fiction, nonfiction, poetry, photography, and interview that sometimes got controversial. More subscribers lived in North Carolina than elsewhere, but the list included plenty of New Yorkers and Californians. Though back then there weren't more than two thousand subscribers, they lived in most every state, and many foreign countries.

One feature of the magazine was a section called

Readers Write, in which readers contributed short pieces on a monthly theme. Giving readers a sense of ownership like that was not only crafty, but proved editorially fresh since the contributors were strong and compelling voices. Anyone reading the magazine and wanting to try their hand at writing for that section could see what to do by reading the current month's entries, and then catching upcoming deadlines, which were six months to a year out. The prompts were simple and effective: "Running Late," "Being Alone," "Keepsakes," "Cash," "Speaking Up," "Security."

They're nothing fancy, but writers have all they need right there, and for one with a sense of play, "Cash," could just as easily lead to a short piece about Johnny Cash or Rosanne Cash as about money.

From New Year's Day to Martin Luther King Day to Valentine's, Mardi Gras, President's Day, St. Patrick's Day, Easter, and beyond: any formal or informal holiday, or any special day such as a birthday or anniversary (my March 2 plane crash anniversary is always good), can get you started — and over the years have almost certainly been used by *The Sun* for that section. And just like for Readers Write contributors, none of us really needs much more than a single word or two to get going if we have the time and inclination since the possibilities are infinite. But once underway, it's also possible to write a sequence of holiday poems, stories, or essays, or expand into something even more grand and ambitious.

Over time, I've not only written poems about holidays and special occasions, I've spent whole holiday weekends writing. Maybe it's because I never had that strong sense of family, but once I found my writing, I've preferred spending holidays like Thanksgiving and Christmas alone with my work.

The week between Christmas and New Year's is particularly good, I think, since it's often free of the usual distractions. For some years now, I've thought of it as the orphan week, and a few years ago, amid a season I was busy with other things and hadn't been writing, I wrote this sonnet, "Winter Bulletin," to better understand what exactly I was thinking:

Winter Bulletin

Once again, orphan week of December,
the six short days from Christmas to New Year's.
Perhaps a long look back to see just where
we've been. What did we do in September,
the early chill of fall? And remember
April, the lengthening light? Did we hear
good news or bad? Are we any nearer
our goals (those mythic and magic numbers)?
It's our orphan week, too, to look ahead,
redeem dreams, solve the relentless future
through hope and list. What's yours? Be a blessed
partner, parent? Live more simply instead?
Perhaps, like me, it's to spurn calendar
and clock, make each speck not better, but best.

I've told the story in chapter 5 about the writing workshop I led back in 1993 during part of that week. While it may have been a success both for myself and my one attendee, Barbara, it certainly didn't draw hordes then, and I doubt a similar event would draw any better now. The pressure from a partner or a family, which for some writers is always a concern, is intensified during holidays. There's never a single way through this. In some relationships, it might be fine to spend those days writing. In others, anathema.

For three years I lived in New York City, with my partner, Rosalind. Our first year together, she flew to California to visit her eldest daughter's family. I stayed in New York, where I wrote a good chunk of a nonfiction manuscript, a draft which I finished that spring. I remain convinced that if I hadn't spent the holiday week alone writing, I'd likely never have finished.

The following year I joined Rosalind and her family for Christmas. And the year after that, our final year together, I let her go off alone, and spent the week in our New York apartment, revising a short story collection, composing the poem about that orphan week, ruminating once more about my future.

I recall a 1989 end-of-the-year conversation with a colleague, an art professor. A visiting professor that year in Sitka, I spent most of the Christmas break holed up in my sublet, writing poems as well as the short story that at last completed the project I'd worked on in graduate school. After writing that short story, I took a day off, then went back to work on the novel I'd started the preceding year.

My colleague said that she too was concentrating on her own work through the Christmas break, and it was her favorite time of year. She told me about her mentor in Oregon, her favorite art professor. This professor and his wife made a ritual of spending holidays in the studio. Accomplished artists, the couple loved their work, and loved each other. They had the best marriage she'd ever seen.

2001, I spent the last two weeks of the year at the Virginia Center for Creative Arts, a residential retreat for working artists in rural Amherst County, across the road from Sweet Briar College. Technically I was a Fellow, as were the other attendees in residence, a group of approximately two dozen writers, visual artists, and composers. I was also on scholarship, which meant instead of paying the requested $100/day, which covered room, board, and miscellaneous expenses, I wrote a check for only a tiny fraction. Fellows came and went throughout my two weeks, depending on the time period we'd been accepted for. All of us had to apply for our fellowships, and we were in various stages of career, from emerging to well-established. One Fellow, whose weeks overlapped with mine, was a professor with a half-dozen books, and had been coming to VCCA annually for years now.

Though I was only paying a few dollars a day, I had my expenses. Like other artist residency programs, the application included an application fee, which was minimal. But for someone applying to several, as some artists do, it can run into hundreds of dollars. For this opportunity, I only learned in August I'd been accepted in, and had already booked an early December job back in Alaska, and planned a recording session around it. That meant I'd have to travel to Virginia from Anchorage, which was going to be expensive. But fellowships like these are special, and when you have the good fortune to be invited, you figure a way to go. There may never be another chance.

One productive Alaska writer I know manages to secure a residency almost every January or February, and has made it an essential part of a writing life. It's a chance to focus wholly on the work and leave winter for several weeks, while enjoying the camaraderie of the other artists in residence. That writer can talk about the differences between various artists' communities.

Though my project in Virginia was to revise a novel, I barely touched it during my two weeks there. Instead I slept an inordinate amount, which I heard was not unusual for first-time Fellows. Though we could eat at any time—and there were some artists I don't believe I saw the whole time I was there because they kept erratic hours—I made sure to eat breakfast and dinner when scheduled in a communal dining area, where I enjoyed meeting the others in residence. Our festive Christmas dinner was appropriately abundant.

We slept in residence halls and worked in assigned studios, where when we opened the front door in the early afternoon, our boxed lunch was there, waiting. Most days, artists were arriving and others were leaving, so there were always new faces, and despite a routine, there was always the sense of the unfamiliar, and the possibility of a surprise. Though none of the friendships I made there have lasted, I met artists I liked, whom I stayed in touch with over the following years. Some evenings, ten or fifteen of us would gather in a parlor and share our work through informal readings, showings, or recitals. A few nights I stayed up late with a scrabble-playing friend.

I wrote six new poems, including three inspired by friendships I'd made there, and composed twenty fiddle tunes. The smartest thing I did was to bring a tape recorder; otherwise, the music would have vanished into the air. Instead, the tunes ended up on my 2006 double CD, *All Originals, All Traditionals*. Every time I listen to the CD of originals, I'm taken back to my two weeks in Virginia, and my studio. Still, as much as I appreciated the fellowship, parts of it felt annoying. It seemed wrong somehow to fly five thousand miles round-trip when I could have stayed in Anchorage, or found someplace at least en route to my next job, and set up a personal retreat since I was disciplined enough to do this on my own—I'd already been doing it for years. Why spend two long days traveling back-and-forth when I was already traveling so much in conjunction with the rest of my work?

When I left for college, I was ecstatic to at last be out of the childhood house. In retrospect, I only wish I'd known enough to have gone further. Durham, North Carolina? Why hadn't I imagined comparable college campuses in Nashville, New Orleans, San Antonio, Evanston, or somewhere out west? Was it any surprise then that I rarely returned, spent my twenties kicking around, working a variety of jobs, growing increasingly estranged from both my mother, who had moved near Miami to be closer to her elderly mother, and my father, who had remarried and remained in Philadelphia? Was it any surprise that I had to move to Seattle, far away from either parent, to at last find my voice? Was it any surprise that I next moved to Alaska, even farther away?

Aside from the auction story, I've written just two other fiction pieces that have even remotely referred to my actual family. But poetry allowed me that space to write. Almost immediately, once I started writing poems, I began writing about my father. In April 1986, I spent a weekend laboring hard on a long poem titled, "The Cure," where the second-person narrator digs a small hole that weeks later has grown mysteriously deep, reinforced with walls, like a mine or a well. Writing the poem, I didn't know where it, or the narrator, was going, but it felt true when the narrator referred to "August:/ your father's burial" and later reminisced about both parents, especially the father, who is described as so cold, so cold/sometimes, your father. A bastard." The poem ends with the narrator shoveling even deeper, hitting water, then scurrying back up to the surface in order to wind the crank of the pulley that had been constructed. Inside the bucket that has been lifted up is "your baby boy."

Good poem? I wouldn't say (and it was among those that caused Professor B to pronounce I was no poet), but it's in one of my collections and I still recall how it totally engaged me in the writing. Rereading it, I consider it a more authentic version of my auction story. I later learned that my father had been in a serious car accident the weekend I spent writing that poem. When I shared the work with my classmate, Elijah, and told him that I'd written it, coincidentally, during a time my father nearly died in a wreck, Elijah only said, *Coincidence? Welcome to poetry.*

There was power there, I understood that, and as I kept writing poems, I continued studying how contemporary poets harnessed that power and handled personal issues. My 1988-1989 year in Juneau, it became my own sick sport, the myriad of ways I could kill off my father in a poem or refer to him as dead. For several years I continued the obsession, sometimes killing my mother instead, occasionally delving into what I imagined of their courtship and marriage, or else exploring the family dynamic in other ways. Though I'd stopped talking to my very-alive mother, and was soon to stop talking to my very-alive father, writing these poems didn't strike me as the least bit grotesque.

Father and Son

To pursue his dream, the father
abandoned a wife, a daughter, and a son
to build a business. Today he lives
in a classy suburb, a fancy house.
Though his second wife dotes, the ex
is shattered, the daughter coasts,
and the son, a writer, practices
the craft of killing his old man off
on paper. Dear old Dad.
The father's been choked, hung,
drowned, knifed. He's suffered
sudden heart attacks, drawn-out
cancers, bad luck in cars.
Neglected as a boy, the son
learned to survive as best he could
by making the imagined, real.
The father, no better or worse,
never had a chance.

Here's another, a sign that I was moving on:

Fairbanks Cabin

My father, lifelong Philadelphian
visiting Alaska, could only see
I drove an old dented van and lived

in a small, mean, low-rent dwelling
with shabby plywood exterior, peeling
front door that couldn't lock, drab
unmatched furniture, faded carpet,
a ladder leading to God only knew.
A house without plumbing where I hauled
water from a spring ten miles away
and sat daily to contemplate digestion
in an outhouse with styrofoam seat.

Father, to have missed the arctic sky
that thrills; the utter privacy
and simplicity that comfort;
the blueberry bushes that feed;
the winter months that teach;
the heater that warms; the loft with desk,
typewriter and mattress that realizes
my dreams. Father, that you traveled
five thousand miles and missed my being
saddens me. I only journey further.
What once had been is elsewhere.

    I once heard someone say that one of the great benefits of writing is giving your characters what you yourself would like to own, but couldn't afford, or maintain. By writing about a certain car or house, you could imagine yourself driving one, or living that lifestyle. By writing about a certain place, you could imagine yourself living there.
    Desperately wanting to cut ties from my parents, I physically moved, then stopped speaking to them. Eventually I wrote poems killing them off.
    Some of the poems were published. Though powerful as those and others might have been, they were only poems. And being a writer only partially identified me. I had good days and bad days, happy times and sad times.

Estranged from my mother, I would go twenty-seven years between visits, from 1984 to 2011. When I saw her, it was as if no time had passed.

Also estranged from my father, I would go twenty-one years, from 1990 to 2011, seeing him two months before he passed on. He'd been in ill health for years and when I saw him, I broke down crying. So old and sick, he looked nothing like I remembered. Yet it was certainly him there in the hospital bed.

Are you still the fiddling poet, he asked, smiling, by way of greeting.

I nodded with tears streaming down my face. When it suits me, I answered.

We spent a few hours together, not saying much, his wife eyeing me suspiciously since they had tried to reach out to me twenty years before when I'd been sick, when my body had mysteriously broken down. But their attempted intervention had only muddled things. My father's way so often was to bully or lecture, and I hadn't needed or wanted that. Nor had I needed or wanted the newer and better medical specialists they'd tried to aim me towards, since I'd already found that my illness had baffled any attempts to be treated by conventional medicine.

So I'd had to go my own peculiar way in order to get well. And I had gotten well, which had also meant dropping things. Difficult family relationships were the easiest to let go of—they were already so tenuous. Later, once more healthy, I started combining the music, writing, teaching, and performance. By then my father and his wife had moved to Florida, near West Palm Beach. They had read my books and my poems, even the ones that had been so hurtful. They had listened to my CDs.

I kept crying.

And in a story so improbable I could never have invented it, my sister, who had stayed in regular contact with both parents, had recently found our still-embittered mother an assisted living home. What our mother didn't know, and would have balked about had she known, was that her wizened ex-husband was in a rehab center a quarter mile from her new unit. The day I visited my mother for the first time in so long, I kissed her cheek, took leave, then drove off, pulling out of the driveway with a left turn, and a few yards down the street, took the first left. I parked in the lot, and called to see if my father would even take my visit.

If I hadn't written so harshly about my parents, I wonder what I might have written instead, or whether I'd have gotten bogged down, and stopped.

Or maybe I was meant to write about my parents, and should have written more. I should have been easier on them, and on myself. But could I have been?

It was William Stafford, my favorite, who has written that when in process of creation he didn't censor himself, and at that early stage didn't concern himself whether a piece of writing was politically correct, or significant in any way. The process of writing was enough. I've tended to agree with most of what he says about writing, and agree with him there too.

Before I found publishers for my books, I self-published 26 chapbooks. One is titled, *Dear Mother, Dear Dad*, its subtitle: *not-so-nice parent poems*. Included are the two epistolary poems which combine to make the chapbook's title—and here's one more assignment: write a poem in the form of a letter to your mother or father. Or write one in the form of a letter to someone else.

It may take awhile, but trust that if you keep at it, the writing will continue to widen and deepen in ways you won't predict. And even if you leave the writing for awhile, when you do come back, that's okay. All's forgiven.

Your writing will be there waiting, like family.

18
Failed Novelist
(Self-Sabotage and Other Sports)

A few weeks after I applied to the writing program in Fairbanks, while still in Seattle, I had the strangest, most vivid dream of my writing life. I woke up with a full-blown story: A Native man was imprisoned for life after an alcohol-related offense—and despite his efforts and the efforts of others who wanted to help, there was nothing any of them could do to change his situation. Those efforts, however, which wouldn't change his situation, *would* change the lives of everyone in his sphere: his lawyer, his fellow prisoners, the prison's staff, his family, even his Native village.

I've never had a dream like it before or since. And once I was accepted to the University of Alaska Fairbanks, I made the writing of that novel my goal for the program. Within weeks I found a job teaching a Creative Writing workshop in the prison. That first semester, taking a class on literary criticism, I wrote my major paper on Ken Kesey's *One Flew Over the Cuckoo's Nest*, the work that would partially model mine. For at least several weeks I was the world's authority on the writer and book. My second semester, in addition to continuing leading the writing workshop in the prison, I also taught a developmental writing class there through the local community college. I felt that I was learning what I needed in order to write the novel.

So many years later, I've yet to start.

Instead I wrote short stories in graduate school, which took time. Writing poems also took time, as did the critical papers for the literature classes. Teaching also took time. As I wrote more stories, I wondered how to best fit them together. The story about the writer-who-didn't-write might have been cliché, made more suspect by an ending where the writer fell sleep drunk and stoned. But it was my cliché to own. The completed story wasn't bad.

I considered the plot more deeply. What if I turned the cliché upside-down and wrote a collection that began with a creation myth—already written!—followed by a story about a couple on a date arguing about which movie to go see (one of the choices is to go see a strange fragmented movie about a writer who doesn't write)—to be written!— and then followed it with the writer-who-doesn't-write story, which I already had. And then what if I followed that story with "the movie fragments," that is all those stories, all complete within themselves, which referred back to the writer-who's-not-writing story. As a result, the stories would all function as "dream" stories: the stories the writer would write if only he was writing. I'd already written some; I only needed to write the rest. Once completed, I'd then only need to write the last three stories: one about the writer awaking, realizing that something was different now; one about the couple walking out of the cinema, discussing the strange fragmented movie they'd just seen; and one with a final end-of-the-world myth.

I spent three years in graduate school and the next two years writing and revising thirty-three total stories for this project. What did I end up with?

A novel?

A short-story sequence?

A mess of a manuscript by someone who had read

too much fiction and graduate school literary criticism?

No matter, though thirteen of the original thirty-three stories have been published, and though I've revised the manuscript yet again, retyping the manuscript from scratch, I learned to write better.

Though the book has yet to find a home (and I've ditched a number of the stories), both the published and unpublished pieces still seem strong to me, as does the concept.

Failed novelist? Failed writer? Something else?

Spring 1989, living in Juneau, in the midst of writing some of the longer stories for that short story manuscript, I wrote one that felt like the story I wrote in Seattle that branded me a writer, only much longer. Within two weeks I had a polished 25,000-word piece of fiction set in Fairbanks. The writing had energized me, and the story had come to a natural close. But there was a problem: it was going to be far too long for the collection. And while it seemed finished enough for a stand-alone novella, it really didn't seem to be that either. I groaned realizing that now I had a real novel to contend with, and needed to do more with it.

Somewhere, the prison story receded further.

The novel took eight years to write, through several moves, a protracted illness, a plane wreck, and a pair of crashed computers. My first memoir recounted attempts to get this published. At one point I came fairly close to an agent, who cautioned me it would not be an easy sell to publishers. Over the years, I've had a variety of readers praise the manuscript, a contemporary relationship story set in Fairbanks, Juneau and Nome around the time when I was living in those places. But the praise feels meaningless. It hasn't come from anyone with the wherewithal to publish the book.

Several years ago when I was living in New York City, down to hard copies of the manuscript, I retyped the complete manuscript, cutting 20,000 words, strengthening it yet again, and started querying once more. A half dozen agents requested the manuscript. Three of them rejected it; the others declined to respond to an email follow-up several months later, asking about the status of the manuscript.

Failed novelist? Failed writer? Something else?

When I moved to New York, I spent six months writing a memoir documenting my bankruptcy, twining a narrative about that process with one that recounted past jobs and the family attitudes that shaped me. The idea was to shed light on what brought on a six-figure credit card debt, and what could be done about it.

Topical, yes?

Alas, I haven't been able to find to interest anyone other than a long-time bookseller in the Pacific Northwest, who read an early draft, before extensive edits, and pronounced that it might be a challenge to sell, but it would sell some, and was an important read.

Failed writer? Something else?

Before the recent run of Donald Trump-related books, and the 2019 acceptance of my collection of sports poems, it had been a decade since I'd had a book of poetry come out. I'm still shopping three: a new and selected collection of predominantly Alaska-set poems; a volume of formal verse; and one titled *Leftovers and Gravy*, which contains, literally, the best of the poems that aren't otherwise called for. Most of all these have previously been in journals. But that hasn't made a difference.

Failed poet? Something else?

Why mention all this? Though I've been doing this for a long time now and have kept going, I still have doubts.

The doubt takes up energy, slowing me. But it also makes it easier to empathize with other writers, and to spot when they're not only battling the usual forces, but also practicing self-sabotage.

Stung by the thoughtless remarks of a teacher, classmate, family member, or friend, they'll stop writing, or stop sending work out for publication. Or maybe they'll quit after one too many rejections from journals, publishers, or agents. Or maybe they're tired, finally, of a world that doesn't seem to care about the quality of the work, of unfair or unfit reviewers, so they retreat into their shells, or lash out at allies.

Are any of us immune?

I wonder how my life might have been different if I'd have written that prison novel when I had the impetus.

I wonder what difference it might have been made if I'd have reached out for and then received more help, found a mentor, written more regularly instead of in great big sporadic bursts, found more timely publication and recognition.

When I wonder what's the point, I return to the work, which means making time for the writing despite all the other demands.

Making time is no small thing. It means sometimes saying no to a partner, or a parent, or a child. It means saying no to music, dancing, socializing, and cooking. It means saying no to television and internet. It means saying no to a cleaner house and a better maintained yard. It means saying no to errands and chores, some of which really shouldn't be delayed or otherwise pushed aside. But by delaying and pushing aside, it means the writing is *not* being delayed, is *not* being pushed aside.

For as long as it takes, it means saying no until the work is done.

It means once the work is done, to make time to begin the next piece of work.

When writers make time to write, no matter the result, no matter the reception, they triumph.

19
Indignities

The middle of my first semester in Fairbanks, one frigid morning I walked between buildings with a classmate, who turned to me and said that in just a few months I'd gained the respect of others in the program since I worked so hard despite not having the talent.

I should have just laughed. I may have had doubts, but after the past year in Seattle I knew I could write, and was sure I had "the talent," or whatever my fellow writer meant by the statement. Instead, I just stood there, slack-jawed and dumbfounded. It wasn't until a year later, when I'd learned enough about crafting poems, and recalled the remark, that I had a means to document the exchange, and get closure.

The Duel

You were pushing open a glass door
and I was trailing when you turned
to say you admired my work ethic
because I didn't have the talent.

You little rooster. I wanted
my hands around your stringy neck.
I didn't move north to write
ordinary stories, or experience

screwy put-downs. We tramped
ten more yards across worn dirty snow,
your ensuing silence cold, blunt,
mean as iron, your breath smoking

like a shotgun. You'd fired first,
and missed. I later targeted pen
on paper, pulled, and hit a snipe
that was, as usual, calling to itself.

What was the comment ultimately about?

I'd never truly know, and resolved to pay closer attention to my surroundings. I'd heard rumors of minor political intrigue throughout the department—after all, colleagues had been covering for Professor A for years—but didn't know it would extend all the way to our second semester Latin American literature class, one that had been beset by problems from near the start. A few weeks into the course, our professor, Professor O, who had been department chair, lost that position in a coup of sorts. Of retirement age, the professor promptly packed up and left Fairbanks for good, leaving our class orphaned. A colleague, Professor P, picked it up two weeks later, but the only time we could meet was three hours on a weekday afternoon. Mine was the only conflict, since that afternoon I was teaching the community college developmental writing class in the prison.

I was asked to drop the class, but balked. The change of time wasn't my fault, I argued, and not only had I attended the first two classes, but over Christmas break had purposely read all the assigned books, so had been especially looking forward to the meetings. As it was, I'd already completed a fair portion of the course work.

My petition was successful, and the new department head, along with Professor P, decided that if I wrote the required papers, plus completed an additional short paper each week in lieu of attending class, and appeared at a final class meeting, which would take place one evening, I'd be permitted to continue the class.

The extra weekly assignments felt heavy-handed—I'd much rather have attended class and not labored over the additional writing—but I was glad for the reprieve, and looked forward to the final meeting, which was at Professor P's apartment, where we drank beer, snacked on pretzels and chips, and went around the room, discussing our final papers. I was next-to-last, and after the easy give-and-take beforehand, launched into a description of my research paper, an examination of Mario Vargas Llosa's *Conversation in the Cathedral*, and how the novel turned on one character, nicknamed Cayo Shithead. It was Professor P, who had been in the background all night, who held up a hand, and asked me a pointed question, an edge in the voice.

I thought I'd answered reasonably, but the professor followed up, making a statement that I wasn't sure was quite accurate, at least from my research. I recalled this professor had virtually no background in the subject—after all, this class had been developed by the departed Professor O—and had taken the overload class as a favor, so I referred back to one of my earlier position papers, which had been deemed satisfactory.

After Professor P asked a third question, half the class suddenly went after me as if on cue, peppering me for a quarter hour. Earlier in the semester, something like this had almost happened to a classmate during the writers' workshop—*almost*, since Professor E squelched that ambush after the first two comments. But this was directed at me, under the seeming command of the professor. I sat there wishing I hadn't started the second beer, and was relieved finally when the grilling was over. I don't recall what happened to the classmate whose paper followed mine, only that I felt numb. Afterward I asked classmates who weren't involved with the questioning whether it was as odd as I remembered. Even odder, they said, nodding.

I was glad to leave that class behind with my B grade, pleased to have made it further along on my path, happy to have been introduced to several Latin American novels that opened me to what was possible. Vargas Llosa, Cortázar, Garcia Márquez, Borges, Fuentes. But that final meeting I've never forgotten, and have sworn never to treat students as I'd been treated.

Creative Writing workshop? Literature class? Composition? Developmental writing? At some point they were all so much the same. How difficult was it to treat attendees equally, respectfully?

In 2003, I housesat for ten weeks at a friend's who was off at a writers' residency. I might have made the stay my own residency—in fact, that was the plan—but got waylaid on a side project. My friend had internet access, and instead of doing my own creative work, I spent several weeks researching every college and university English Department in the country, and contacting writers who I thought might be interested in hosting me. The creative work, though necessary, didn't directly translate to income. I needed money.

I picked up several jobs for the following year, made some lasting friends, and established a procedure I use to this day. Now, several weeks before performing near a campus, I'll contact the school's writers, and invite them to my event, offering to comp them if appropriate, and mention how I presume they all have friends, colleagues, students who would be interested in some of what I do. I send them a paragraph or two with the details of my scheduled program, which also introduces them to my work.

If I were teaching, I know I'd appreciate the head's up, and would spread the word.

But I'm not teaching, and it doesn't always work like I envision. Sometimes one of these professors will respond that they're sorry but their department schedules visiting writers a year or more out so can't accommodate my request. When I get one of these, I'll reread my initial email and see that, no, it's just as I've thought: I've made no such request. Last year, one professor even tersely wrote back: We're not going to have you to our campus. It's never going to happen.

Sometimes I'll reply, repeating the initial announcement, gently correcting the mistaken impression. Other times I'll just shake my head. In spring 2004, I performed at a small concert venue near a big state university, one with an MFA program, and a professor I contacted must have been intrigued, since he attended the show with several students. There had been a good turnout, and it felt like a successful evening. Afterward the professor introduced himself, congratulated me both on my ingenuity and on the event, then shook his head.

I'm glad I came, but just so you know, this kind of thing doesn't work on our campus. We don't bring street poets.

Street poets? I eyed him curiously. What do you mean?

We bring academic poets.

I looked at him. I had two books then, both with a well-established independent press, both distributed by a university press. In the next three years, I didn't know it yet, but would have four more books. But even then my work had been published in hundreds of literary journals, many affiliated with colleges and universities, maybe in some of the exact ones this professor had also published in. Street poet? I'd written and published all kinds of poems, including formal poems. In some places, formal poetry is considered as academic as it gets.

But in his mind, presumably because I played fiddle and drew a decent audience of paying attendees, there you have it, a street poet. Or, just as likely, maybe it was because although I had my MFA, I wasn't currently a full-time faculty member at another institution.

Regardless, there was going to be no arguing.

For years I'd thought it was the quality of the work

that was paramount. And for years I'd been wrong. Maybe there was just too much clutter, too much high-quality work. But this wasn't a question of clutter. Taste can always be debated, but this was something else. People who are inclined to say no will find their reasons.

The following year I attended a reading in Anchorage by a former classmate who had published a novel, which I had read and enjoyed. Happy for the classmate's success, and, yes, a little bit envious of it, I also secretly hoped that the success might in some small way make it easier for my own novel to be published.

Afterward, I spoke with the writer. The past years I'd been touring, I explained, and in the process had been going around and meeting people. If there was anything I could do to help, I said, just let me know.

My ex-classmate just looked at me. I've seen your posters all over town. It looks like you're just trying to be famous for being famous.

I stood there and stared. Had I somehow been transported back ten years, time-traveled to a prior classmate, a prior put-down?

Having posters that were noticed all over Anchorage wasn't such a bad thing, I might have said if I wanted to start a good-natured debate. After all, I was doing several events in the coming weeks and the posters were up to help with promotion.

Famous for being famous? What the fuck are you talking about? I might have sputtered if I wanted to start an argument. Then I might have gotten defensive and explained that since 2000 I'd had two books come out and three CDs. Plus I'd already recorded one more CD, part of a planned 2-CD set, and a publisher had promised another poetry collection in 2006. Public events were my livelihood, and the past four years I've driven across country a half dozen times, so what is it you're trying to say?

But I just stood there. The classmate was obviously

not going to be interested in my immediate help, or anything I might offer in the future.

Indignities? Worse was several years later, when I was simply trying to get my Alaska-set children's book in stores throughout the state. Though self-published, within three months the book was picked up for distribution by University of Alaska Press, and came with a music CD, which made it an especially attractive package. Though I'd been successful getting both the book and CD in a number of shops, I hoped for more. The following year, because I'd be performing just down the road, I tried to set up a signing at the Denali National Park gift shop. The store manager referred me to the manager of an Anchorage-based organization that contracted services at dozens of park gift shops and information centers throughout the state. The Anchorage manager then referred me back to the Denali Park store manager.

I'd been playing this game with these same folks for years with little success. I'd have thought having my children's book affiliated with the state's university press would have finally made a difference, but it didn't, and according to others I wasn't the only one frustrated with this particular bureaucracy.

When the manager of the park store finally responded to my query, it was to say that though my interest was appreciated, the store had a mission to stock books specific to the place, so couldn't find a place for mine, or honor my request for a signing.

I wrote back that *D is for Dog Team* was a book with a second front cover: *D is for Denali*. Kudos, I said, for staying local, but please realize almost half the acrostic poems in the book could refer specifically to the region in and around the national park, and the rest are all Alaska set. Denali is your park. Dog mushing is local. Can you reconsider?

Fine enough that I never heard back, but when I

stopped by the shop later that summer since I was already nearby, I took a good look around. Unfortunately the manager wasn't in, so I couldn't introduce myself. But it was easy to notice that the selection of children's books and CDs were identical to most every store in the state—a mix that included excellent ones (some local, some not) and some that seemed decidedly run-of-the-mill. However, the general trade books were more eclectic. I couldn't help noticing the poetry collection by Mary Oliver, from New England, and the essays by Kentucky writer, Wendell Berry. I left the manager a note saying I was sorry not to meet when I was there, was happy to see the store, but would appreciate an explanation how Mary Oliver and Wendell Berry, as wonderful as they were, fit the shop's mission of stocking Alaska-set books.

I left another copy of the children's book and CD, and a copy of my second poetry collection, distributed by University of New Mexico Press, which featured lots of Alaska-set poems of the natural world. I explained that I'd sent all these to the Anchorage manager previously, but now having seen first-hand the store's interests, maybe these could could be reconsidered.

A day later I received an email from the Anchorage manager, accusing me of a fomenting conspiracy theories.

Conspiracy? That wasn't my word, I answered, thoroughly confused at the language.

After one more tense email exchange, I let it go. The University of Alaska Press could give it their best shot to get the children's book and CD in the stores the Anchorage-based organization managed. Despite the Alaskan setting, my general poetry collection didn't have a chance there. I knew my work wasn't going to change the world. But it had value, took up little retail space, and should have been considered local virtually everywhere the state. Because I'd once stopped by the bookstore in the Anchorage airport and left a copy of my first book, *Nome Poems*, the manager took a good look, decided to display it, and sold a copy or two a week for the length of her employment. But that had been one of the success stories. At Denali National Park, I'd only been in touch because I was going to be virtually across the street anyway.

Fomenting conspiracy theories?

Years later, I'm still shaking my head.

And a final anecdote.

At one point, I queried four people at an exclusive New England boarding school: first, a poetry-writing chaplain I'd met at a conference; then the director of student activities, to whom the chaplain referred me; then the outgoing head of the English Department, a novelist, to whom the activities director referred me; then the incoming English Department head, to whom the outgoing head referred me. It had taken two solid months to wend my way through, and I'd sent almost a dozen emails, plus three packets by postal mail. I hardly lavished this much care for every potential gig, but once a process had begun, I liked to see it through.

When the incoming English Department head quickly responded to my last email query, congratulating me on my obvious success as an entertainer/singer/poet, but that the interests of the department were going in other directions, I took a deep breath. He'd struck a nerve. It was tempting to reply just as quickly to wonder how a gentleman who taught literature and prided himself on his reading and critical thinking abilities could think I was a successful singer. Nowhere had I ever claimed I sang, and in fact the past few years had incorporated some singing into my events as an extended joke (on stage I'll explain how in elementary school I was assigned to the speaking choir, and how at a former restaurant job I was banned from singing Happy Birthday because I would ruin the tips) to prove that in Alaska anyone can do anything, whether fiddle or write. Or sing, badly. And what kind of successful "poet" did he think I was if in his mind it followed my "success" as "a singer."

It would have been rude to so belabor the issue, but so

temporarily satisfying.

It would have wiser, perhaps, to just let the whole thing go.

Instead I waited a few hours to write him, copying his three colleagues. I thanked him for thinking I was a successful singer, which I wasn't because I didn't sing, not really, but was glad he thought so. I wrote that while others have called me "an entertainer," and "entertaining" because I can play fiddle at a high level and can talk on stage in ways that command attention, I always called myself an educator because the music and storytelling were in service to the teaching. I added that contemporary poetry was so often misunderstood. I reiterated that I had only been in touch because I'd met one of his colleagues, had successfully visited similar schools (and myself had graduated from a country day school many years before), and was going to be nearby in the coming year. I was truly sorry I wouldn't be able to share my talents.

I read it over once, twice, three times, then pressed "send." I didn't think this particular lesson would sink in, but I was a teacher, so would see it through.

And with that I went on with the work.

20
21 Sentences
(A Narrative Guide)

Instead of using individual words from the dictionary as prompts, we can use phrases or sentences. Really, it's similar to when we created a character from the names. Once we chose that name, the descriptive phrases came from answering questions, which could vary without limit.

Years ago I stumbled into one of my best stories using a version of the following 21-sentence prompt to get started. There was no reason, of course, it couldn't have led into a poem. And though I've written above, parenthetically, this is a narrative guide, there's no reason it couldn't be a guide to lyrics. This time around, I ended up with a poem. It could just as easily have become prose.

1: Write a five-word sentence beginning with the word "You."
2: Write a sentence that includes a body part.
3: Write a sentence that includes a color.
4: Write a sentence that is a question.
5: Write a ten-word sentence that includes a number.
6: Write a sentence that includes either the word "soap" or the word "cup."

7: Write a sentence that includes a shape.
8: Write a sentence that includes somebody speaking.
9: Write a sentence that includes some kind of food.
10: Write a sentence that includes a contraction.
11: Write a sentence that includes an animal.
12: Write a sentence of exactly eight words.
13: Write a sentence that includes the word "dream."
14: Write a sentence of exactly two words.
15: Write a sentence that includes two commas and a metaphor or simile.
16: Write a sentence of at least sixteen words.
17: Write a sentence that includes a proper name (and used as a name).
18: Write a sentence that include the name of a room.
19: Write a sentence that's either a fragment or breaks a rule of grammar.
20: Write a sentence of exactly five words.
21: Write a sentence that ends with the word "you."

One possible result:

You think you've done it. Easy,
like one foot after another,
or calling the gray sky *gray*.
It's black and white, isn't it?
Isn't it? You go into a pocket,
pull two five-dollar bills.
Just like that, easy as a cup
of soup. Or a square of butter.
Dinner, you hear. And you think
the chowder excellent, the best
you've had in years. Clams,
mussels, scallops, cod. You lick
your lips after each creamy
spoonful. This is no dream.
No dream. This is your life,
your real and dream-like life,
unfolding like a chair.

> So you sit, take it all in,
> the smells, the tastes,
> the soup, the table, the awful
> and beautiful gray sky.
> Mark, you hear, and turn,
> though Mark isn't your name.
> You're not in a dining room,
> though you were, or so
> you thought. A memory?
> A dream maybe, but not.
> Perhaps it's just a voice
> from the past, or future,
> that has come to greet you.

I don't know where this came from exactly, but it felt like a profitable hour, inventing these particular instructions for the twenty-one sentences (which, once again, could have been eleven, thirteen, seventeen, or twenty-seven sentences with completely different instructions), and then letting each of them have their way.

Let Them Have Their Way, I thought, having reread the last sentence, and I had a working title for a piece which thoroughly engaged me in the writing, and which I can revise to Having Your Way or You Can Have Your Way, and keep the second-person voice.

Was it any good?

Good? That wasn't for me to say yet, and feel like I'm echoing William Stafford, who wouldn't pronounce such a thing at such a time.

But even at this point, the earliest draft, one achieved by running through twenty-one sentences, I can say I've got the start of something. And this was different, much different, than anything I've written lately.

And wasn't that the point?

21
Table For One
(Under House Arrest)

I'm writing this sentence on August 25, 2019. I first "finished" this manuscript in spring 2013, after beginning it mid July 2012. What's different now is that I have a publisher for this, so the work can get out in the world in early 2020.

Writing this has been similar to other projects, but different, too. It has been on my list, this book, but my list is long. I have those six unpublished manuscripts to tinker with and several new projects to begin. And there's the day-to-day routine. On tour, I'm traveling and busy with the logistics that ensure successful days before audiences. When not on tour, I'm dealing with some of those same logistics, and so many others. Each booking is a separate job, and job-hunting means there are *always* emails and phone calls to attend. And if I delay too long, a potential opportunity can disappear for several months, a year, two years, or, in some cases, forever. True, there are *always* new opportunities. But which to pursue? And when? Some colleagues buy computer software and design elaborate systems to help manage this part of their business. Because there are always so many variables, I have a different model, relying on personal contact and staying the course. Not that it necessarily helps. I have people on my short list to call and email who I've regularly phoned and written for nine months now, and *still* haven't reached. But that's okay. Sometimes that's what happens to me, and for any of us pursuing these kinds of jobs. Maybe I'll reach them in month number ten.

Back in summer 2012 I had time free after leaving New York City and my relationship there. I'd gone back to Louisiana, and was staying with a friend, an accordion player who the past year had moved to Breaux Bridge, the small town I'd previously lived, down the road from Lafayette. My friend was renting a spacious double-wide trailer on a dead-end street, an easy walk from downtown. He expected to be gone most of July and August, so was happy to have me in the space. Already he'd offered me closet space for my boxes, which I'd taken him up on. All May I'd been mailing books and CDs via media rate.

My plan back south was to play lots of music, reintegrate myself into the arts community, and plow ahead with the endless work of booking dates. I was sure I'd at last have time for the four poetry manuscripts I wanted to revise again, but didn't think I'd do more writing than that. However, my second week in Louisiana, practicing, stretching to play notes I didn't usually play, I strained my left ring finger. The next weeks, taking care of the injury as best I could, icing regularly, occasionally testing what I could do, the finger worsened dramatically, and my left pinkie also started aching. I passed time working long days on the computer, including making those poetry revisions.

I wasn't sure what exactly had happened since I wasn't using the fingers for typing, and wasn't playing for more than a few minutes when I did take out the fiddle or mandolin. My body's reaction was so different than recent past years when I'd similarly tweaked a finger, wrist, forearm, or shoulder, and quickly healed. This time, I recalled the summer exactly twenty years before, when an April elbow injury had led to systemic joint pains, and a three-year disease process that changed my life.

Though this didn't seem nearly so severe, I sensed I still might be in some trouble. The end of July I was supposed to go to a music festival in West Virginia, which wasn't an official job, but where I'd play music and do the networking that was helpful for my work. Though August was free, beginning in September, I'd be busy through the first week of December. While I had enough money to get through comfortably until my next round of touring, I didn't have *that* much money, and absolutely needed the income from that touring for my next round of expenses.

Canceling dates was out of the question. Come September, if I had to play with only two fingers, I'd figure something, but hoped that wouldn't be the case. Health insurance? I hadn't had a policy of any kind since teaching in Nome twenty years earlier. The Seattle naturopath I'd been seeing since 1993 was my line of defense.

Mid July, three weeks after I'd first hurt myself, I had a bad night. The week before I'd seen a doctor about my finger, and he'd suggested a cortisone shot. I'd been reading about various remedies, and while an injection might have given temporary relief from what had become a deep and persistent pain, cortisone could sometimes worsen problems by masking them. So I'd declined the shot and instead continued with the ice. I also started taking herbal supplements, and taped the ring finger to the pinkie in order to minimize movement, at least until the latest round of inflammation subsided. I also made an appointment for a phone consult with my naturopath, and began seeing a local acupuncturist twice a week.

The bad evening, cooking dinner, I picked up the cutting board wrong, and felt a sharp pain in my injured ring finger. I cried out, cursing. On the computer later, because of the new pain, I felt for the first time as if I could no longer use my left hand at all. And even my right hand felt more fragile.

That was the night I shut the computer down, took a pen out of my pocket, found an old notebook, opened to a clean page, and wrote on top, Chapter 1. Then I began to describe how I used an icebreaker exercise when leading writing workshops. I wrote late into the night, and the writing soothed me. The next day my left hand didn't feel much better, but didn't feel worse, and again I wrote for hours in the notebook, continuing the thread from the night before.

Over the next several days, I made a routine of it, writing in the notebook, describing the evolution and practice of several of the writing exercises I used. Though my finger still hurt, it had calmed enough so I could cook without incident, and could type with my thumbs. This writing didn't feel joyous, but, rather, necessary, a way to survive one particularly long, lonely, sweltering Louisiana week. Over two more days I typed what I'd written—a draft of the first three chapters of this manuscript here, almost 10,000 words—and shut the project down.

Past crisis, I rode to West Virginia with friends, where I didn't play music at the festival, but spent the week visiting many more friends. August, back in Louisiana, I continued with appointments and prepared for my fall tours. Unsure how I'd be able to play—or even whether I'd be able to play—I adapted by narrowing my repertoire to a dozen tunes I could manage adequately with just two fingers. It wasn't much fun having to fiddle this way, but I was grateful to pick up the instrument at all. Surprisingly, though a busy fall and early winter I continued to be well-received both in schools and at public events. It certainly wasn't virtuosity that was the draw, though by carefully choosing tunes within my current limitations, and in some cases having terrific accompanists, I didn't have to do much more than be careful not to overdo.

It took several more months, and a number of temporary setbacks, for the finger to heal. And though I'd only written occasional poems throughout that next year, I'd never stopped thinking of the new manuscript. Late April 2013, back in Louisiana after a short Midwest tour, I had two free months before a job in Texas, and then additional touring in July and August. My boxes were still at my friend's in the double-wide trailer. But all May and into June I'd be staying at another friend's several blocks away, a glass artist who also had a spare bedroom, and could use the extra rental income. The accordion player and the glass artist, who were casual friends, joked that they were sharing me for a season.

My bedroom at the glass artist's was comfortable and private, and after spending two weeks taking care of various chores, I spent the next three weeks under what I've called house arrest. I'd rarely go outside, rarely even left the bedroom and the bed, which I used as my makeshift desk, sitting cross-legged in front of the computer.

I'd been aiming for 2,000 words a day, and for three weeks I'd been almost averaging it. Each day I go back to what I've previously written, tightening it. I thought that if I could finish with a manuscript between 45,000-50,000 words, and then add a full-length collection of writing-related poetry, I had a book. Approaching 35,000 words, knowing I was nearing my goal, I spent the day writing an introduction, which I partially scavenged from a statement of teaching philosophy I'd written for several job applications. That same evening I spent hours researching publishers that might be interested in a book like this. At that stage I was always optimistic. And why not for this project? People take creative writing classes, and this book could help them. People not only read books like this about writing. They buy them.

The next weeks I stayed caught up with my emails and phone calls, confirming several new jobs from Massachusetts to Arizona. When I wanted a break, I went to websites where I could lose myself in any number of ways. For more than three decades I'd prided myself on not owning a television. But now that a computer allowed me to watch or read virtually anything, I no longer bragged I didn't have a TV. Some of those nights that season I even wandered into the living room to watch television with my glass artist landlord, who liked to unwind by viewing favorite programs after finishing the day's projects. I'd bring my dinner, sit across the room on a couch, and watch while I ate.

Mostly I was grateful to have been left alone in a small dark room, my computer for company.

Party? Yes. And no.

This part of it has been a table of one.

Maybe I could have done as well at an artists' retreat, but unless I'd have been offered a sizable stipend, I couldn't have done it as cheaply or efficiently. It costs time and money to attend one. Here, I traveled less than a half mile, and had everything I needed. And the rent was minimal.

There's also no way around it that at some point a writer has got to spend the time producing work. It was one thing to have had a good day of writing. But it was another thing to have a second day, then a third, then a fourth. I stopped going out, except for absolute essentials. I remember an envelope that had been on my bureau there that I'd been meaning to put in the mail. It had been sitting there for a week and a half. That two-mile round-trip walk to the post office was one of the routines I'd been skipping. I knew I ought to exercise more, but that would come. I'd been hard at it, so that in addition to the prose, I composed several of the poems that were in this manuscript.

In New York City, I once ditched a Christmas week with my partner, Rosalind, her three children, and two grandchildren in order to stay home alone and write. One June, fourteen years ago, in the country outside Opelousas, I rented a three-bedroom house approximately thirty miles from where I wrote this. There, I composed five single-spaced pages a day. The end of the month I had a 95,000-word draft of a manuscript that was published three years later. That same month I also made up more than 60 new fiddle tunes.

Now *that* was a residency to emulate.

For this book project, which has taken seven years to ultimately find a publisher, I'm not complaining.

My novel initially took eight years to write. Twenty-two years after "finishing" it, I'm still tinkering with it, so it's been thirty years and counting. No, that kind of writing process isn't for me. I've long learned I'd rather be in one place, and have the time to mow through a project in six months, or less.

This hasn't been ideal, but it could have been worse. Much worse.

Having gotten this far, I have everything I need.

22
A Party of Resources
(Two Books, Six Websites,
Thirty-Four Poems)

With all the good books and websites available to explore, the problem quickly becomes narrowing the list. Reading is essential for writers. But reading to the exclusion of writing is *never* the idea if you're aspiring to write. That kind of reading is a favorite pastime for self-saboteurs. Still, any good book will lead directly and indirectly to so many others. Below are two books (with references to several others) and six websites that are in no way of comprehensive, but will get you started.

The poems? They're mine and are about reading, writing, and writers.

The University of Michigan Poets on Poetry series has published 123 titles over the past 41 years, and William Stafford's *Writing the Australian Crawl*, published in 1978, was the inaugural. "A Way of Writing" a short essay from that book, is a piece I try to somehow include in every workshop I facilitate. 1988-1990, after I graduated from Fairbanks, and was deep in my poetry self-study, I read many of the early books from this series, including one by Alaskan writer, John Haines, and others by

Galway Kinnell, Donald Hall, Robert Bly, Maxine Kumin, and Philip Levine. as well as a second Stafford book, *You Must Revise Your Life*. Now, as in so many things, I'm behind in my reading, including getting to a more recent pair of Stafford books in the series. A Stafford quote: "If I put down something, that thing will help the next thing come, and I'm off. If I let the process go on, things will occur to me that were not at all in my mind when I started. These things, odd or trivial as they may be, are somehow connected. And if I let them string out, surprising things will happen. If I let them string out . . . Along with initial receptivity, then, there is another readiness: I must be willing to fail."

Seattle's literary center, Hugo House, is named after the late Northwest writer and teacher, Richard Hugo. A long-time Boeing Corporation employee, where he began as a technical writer, he left his final position there when he was in his early 40's, two years after his first poetry collection was published. For the rest of his life he taught at the University of Montana. A beloved teacher, he published seven poetry collections, a mystery, and a book of essays, *The Triggering Town*, a book that wasn't in the Michigan Poets on Poetry series, but easily could have been. I reread this one occasionally, and always come away with something useful. Here's a Hugo quote from the second paragraph of the first chapter: "Every moment, I am, without wanting or trying to, telling you to write like me. I hope you learn to write like you. In a sense, I hope I don't teach you to write but how to teach yourself how to write."

Two books? I'll briefly mention another seven (and could easily mention a dozen more): *The Poet's Companion* by poets Kim Addonizio and Dorianne Laux, a 1997 book that includes numerous writing prompts, and an extensive annotated bibliography that was the state of the art at the time; *The Practice of Poetry: Writing Exercises from* Poets Who Teach by poets Robin Behn and Chase Twichell, a 1992 book that feels current with a wide array of exercises, with accompanying short essays—the prompt shared by the late Arizona poet, Jim Simmerman, feels similar to one of mine; *The Portable MFA in Creative Writing*, a textbook that explains five genres—fiction, poetry, creative nonfiction, playwriting, and screenwriting; *Show & Tell*, a textbook from the highly-regarded MFA program at University of North Carolina Wilmington with essays by the writers who teach there; Annie Lamott's *Bird by Bird*, a popular guide to writing (and living); Natalie Goldberg's *Writing Down the Bones*, another popular guide to writing (and living), where one bit of advice is to make a writing date with a friend—which is one way to always make an intimate party out of writing; and John Gardner's *The Art of Fiction* (you could also try his *On Becoming a Novelist*).

Do I recommend any of these unequivocally, including the books by Stafford and Hugo? No one book will ever do everything and some books may not do much of anything, at least not the first time through. Though writing is often solitary, this work doesn't exist in a vacuum. It's not unlike what Professor F said to me more than twenty-five years ago concerning how to process workshop comments. If a single point raised by a single one of these authors leads to a single practical insight you can adopt for your writing, you're ahead. If a single writing exercise leads to one new good piece of writing, you're ahead. If any of these books otherwise inspires or resonates with your writing life, you're ahead.

In addition to the books, the websites below have useful information for writers.

www.pw.org is the online home for *Poets & Writers*, where front and center on the homepage defines their work: "The nation's largest nonprofit organization serving creative writers."

The bimonthly print magazine is an invaluable resource (confession: I haven't subscribed for years because to stay current amid my touring I want the latest in my hands, so buy copies while on the road). In addition to an extensive directory of credentialed writers (to qualify you need to verify a minimum number of publications in a genre, or live events for performance poets), there are numerous resources for writers: information about publication opportunities, residencies, and grants, plus there's a forum for writers to correspond on virtually any writing-related topic.

www.awpwriter.org will take you to all things AWP, an acronym for the Association of Writers and Writing Programs. Front and center on the website, you learn that "AWP provides communities, opportunities, ideas, news, and advocacy for writers and teachers of writing."
Just as MFA programs expanded from the handful that were around in 1967, when AWP was founded, to the more than 250 programs in existence today, so has AWP grown, and there are over 500 member organizations, which include graduate schools, undergraduate schools, and community college Creative Writing programs. The past years the annual conference has surpassed over 12,000 attendees. There are hundreds of sessions over three days, evening readings by well-established writers, and the conference bookfair is the largest of its kind. A connection I made at the Atlanta conference bookfair in 1996 directly led to the publication of my first two books. Connections I made at conferences the past several years in Minneapolis, Los Angeles, Washington DC, Tampa, and Portland directly led to events, and also helped me find a publisher for my collection of sports poems.

In addition to information about the annual conference, the AWP website has a comprehensive guide to current job openings for writers, teachers, and editors, and offers some of the same resources that Poets & Writers offers. The organization's emphasis will always be on schools with MFA programs and their professors and graduates, but the information is useful for anyone looking to go deeper with their writing.

Founded in 1953, *The Paris Review*, has been perhaps the foremost literary quarterly of the era. *www.theparisreview.org/interviews* is the online archive for what has been a distinguishing feature of the magazine: in-depth, intelligent interviews.

During times I've had a budget for journals, I'd pick up a *Paris Review* because in addition to the poetry and prose, there were those interviews, which were always worth the price of an issue. Penguin used to publish anthologies of selected interviews, and over the years I've bought, lent, and bought again some of those anthologies. Now the interviews are available online, and the format is going strong into a seventh decade.

Some representative interviews from the archives: the 50's, William Faulkner and James Thurber; the 60's, Jorge Luis Borges and Vladimir Nabokov; the 70's, Pablo Neruda and Eudora Welty; the 80's, Raymond Carver and Tennessee Williams; the 90's, Toni Morrison and Alice Munro; the 00's, Joan Didion and Norman Mailer; the 10's, Louise Erdrich and John McPhee. The whole list is considerable, and the past week for fun I've (re)read interviews of Jack Kerouac, Ken Kesey, Hunter S. Thompson, Raymond Carver, and Henry Miller. That reading has helped spark a pair of new poems.

In 1977, poet Alberta Turner edited a book, *50 Contemporary Poets: the Creative Process*. Turner interviewed fifty poets of that time and asked them good, commonsense questions about one of their poems. It's like the *Paris Review* interviews, but specific to a particular poem.

For a decade now, contemporary poet, Brian Brodeur, has taken that same good idea and applied it to today's practicing poets. At *www.howapoemhappens.blogspot.com* there are more than 230 poets discussing one of their poems, and the list includes a wide range of well-known

(Robert Hass, Dorianne Laux, Robert Pinsky) and not-so-well-known poets.

Start anywhere: it's a valuable project.

Atlanta-based writer and editor, Robert Lee Brewer has long been keeping a blog that includes numerous interviews and a weekly prompt for poems (which Brewer does himself, and which can often be adapted for prose). *www.writersdisgest.com/editor-blogs/poetic-asides* and you'll notice Brewer is affiliated with Writer's Digest, which is another resource, and publishes a monthly magazine, and a plethora of books to help writers. These prompts from Brewer: write a poem that has to do with child's play; write a poem that is about something or somebody that is unplugged, whether literally or metaphorically; write a poem that has to do with being late, and again, this can be taken literally or metaphorically (which, if you're darkly ambitious, could be a reason to write an epitaph, for yourself or another, or to bring someone back from the dead).

I'd planned to end at five websites, but since resources are everywhere, while I was initially writing this chapter I received an email, clicked a link, and came across *www.selfmadewriter.blogspot.com* from Alaskan writer, Deb Vanasse. Several years ago Deb Vanasse and Andromeda Romano-Lax, another Alaskan writer, joined to form a blog, 49 Writers, which quickly became the go-to resource for all information about contemporary Alaskan writing. Since most newspapers have long stopped publishing regular features about the book trade and literary arts, the blog was a success, and soon led to a literary center of the same name, which has also been a success.

In January 2012, in addition to many other projects, Vanasse began a new blog to document her own work and concerns. She posting weekly for awhile, calling herself a self-made writer, and explained on the home page that this is "A teaching series for writers." Under the "Try This" section were numerous prompts. Here's one: Give your characters something to fight over. Here's another: Rewrite something you're working on in the voice of an author you admire. Now, as I revise this, I see Deb's life and work has evidently evolved. She's now at *http://coastwriting.org/writers-journey-blog/*. It's still a useful resource.

In the end, yes, we've all got to do on our own what we've got to do.

But we're also all in this together. If you want help, it's out there. Websites, books, workshops, conferences, schools, personal coaches, friends, family.

Get to it, and keep at it.

Me, I next have poems about writing to share. Maybe that's a way in for you, the reader, to be further inspired.

To an Apprentice Writer

Everything's been written
(just look at the books).

So easy to quit
when every wilderness

has been mapped,
every love story launched,

every household built
(though that hasn't stopped others).

I only mean to say
go on with the work.

Not yet has everything
been written by you.

Poems

Temporary homes
of image and sound
inexplicable as a tent

that contains bedroom,
closet, trapdoor, fumes,
stairs, basement, a human
exploring ancestral ruins.

Graphology

Learning cursive,
she practices
letting the pencil
fly by itself
lightly on white
unlined paper,
allows the lead
to shape a soft
illegible scrawl
of a signature,
writes the story
of someone wholly new —
eight-year-old doc
on her first
girl rounds.

Author at Nine

He'd fall asleep,
his nose in a book,
and in his dreams
blunderbuss,
callipygous,
Galapagos, or so
he told his parents.

He was, they agreed,
an eccentric child.

Walt Whitman's Visit

When Walt Whitman visited, he tracked mud on the
 living room carpet, slurped soup at the dinner table,
 picked up a chicken drumstick with his hands, ate it
 to the bone, gnawed at its marrow, licked his knife
 after he buttered his bread, farted with gusto,
 at my mother, did not apologize.

My mother was a proper lady. She told Walt Whitman to
 leave early the next morning, or she'd call the police.

The next morning Walt Whitman woke me at daybreak
 and took me outside to the yellowpink sunrise.
There he sat me on the grass, sat himself next to me, held
 hand, and sang me his rhapsody, the song of God's
 lattice.
He chanted about the giganticness of insects, the foot
 traffic of animals, the flight of sparrows over the
 midwest expanse;
He chanted about the greedy bluegrass and the purple
 prairies, the weedsy lands and the swamps, the
 thousands of reeds swaying in the wind beside a New
 Hampshire pond;
He chanted about the salmon, the crab, the lobster, the
 catfish;
He chanted about Jupiter, Neptune, and the boyhood
 dream of Vulcan, his world frozen but for a single
 blossoming pear tree, its leaves shooting;
He chanted about politics, the gala bashes of governors
 and kings, the orchids and roses, the menus of
 turkeys and veal, the toasts to debauchery;
He chanted about the proliferation of cities, the spans of
 bridges, the hammers and chisels men and women
 used to build churches, schools, courthouses, hospitals;
He chanted about the cracks in windows, the leaks in
 roofs, the warp in floors, the holes that cannot be filled;

He chanted about the man and woman who fell in love
  forever and had it end after two years;
He chanted about the paternity of sunlight, its rays
  striking all;
He chanted about the mother who understood, and the
  mother who did not.

For some time I listened to Walt Whitman's picturebook
  of chants.

I saw praying mantises bathing in lagoons, a wolfpack
  lazing in a field of flowers, a single eagle circling a
  Minnesota farm;
I saw roads and rivers, the roadways and riverways all
  leading to alpine meadows where sheep grazed in
  pairs, where bears pawed blueberried hillsides, where
  every December the snow fell and fell, and no one
  knew how deep;
I saw a chasm, bottomless, and on the near side
  hundreds of palm trees grew like beanstalks, and on
  the far side a smoke-spewing volcano foretold rain;
I saw a navy of sharks, led by an octopus, swim by the
  rotted hull of an English warship;
I saw a bugler with his cheeks puffed out, his eyes shut,
  his fingers wrapped tight around his horn;
I saw stained glass windows, a dark room, a casket
  draped with the American flag;
I saw the full moon rise, and a steeple puncture it;
I saw a squadron of bats fly over the city like migrating
  geese, like Halloween stuntplanes, like the Luftwaffe;
I saw two photographs:one of my father in a soldier's
  uniform; the other of my mother as a seventeen-year-
  old bride, a big smile on her face;
I saw my father die in France on my first birthday, his left
  leg severed at the knee;
I saw my mother grieve, her grief increasing each year.

When I woke, the robins, the cardinals, and the orioles were singing; the lawn, the bushes, and the trees were singing. Walt Whitman, gone, sang no longer, and under sunny birdcries I crawled across the lawn, past the dried and split birch and oak, past the ax and maul leaning against the block, towards the dirtpile. After crawling to the top, I began digging a hole, shoveling the dirt with my hands. Sometime that afternoon it started to drizzle, a mist that eased the digging. I dug, and kept sinking until evening.

When my mother called me to dinner, I didn't appear, and when she called again and again, my last name my father's name, I dug harder, burrowing deeper into the muddy earth.

Going Pubic

Next time you look for a pen,
try standing naked before
your full-length mirror,
and put your right third finger
to your mouth. Wet the tip
as if tongue-kissing a wick,
then watch yourself draw a line
through the brow, between the eyes,
down the middle of the nose,
the lips, the throat, the chest,
navel, abdomen, into the hair,
the genitals, inside yourself,
to blood, bone, sizzle, spit.
Look. Writers must live in this
public place where the ink
is self and the sex burns —
like masturbation with dynamite.

A Short Story Formula

Contrived balance won't
fly in an unsettled,
fractious universe.

For more lift, shift
distance and weight.
Write what matters

as if it doesn't.

Toss sandbags from balloons.

Flophouses

The fat front desk clerk with bad skin
sneezed, wiped his nose on his sleeve,
then said he guessed he'd have a room
in an hour: $29 a night, plus tax.
Sold, I said, without having to look,
calculating I could stay five nights,
save $400 because though this was
no fancy downtown convention hotel,
it couldn't be worse than the Boston room
with cockroaches, the Philly room
with cigar smoke, the Pittsburgh room
with mildewed sheets, the Detroit room
with clogged toilet down the hall,
the Chicago room surrounded
by scufflers and brawlers—one night
ending with sirens at 4 A.M. Here,
cheaply, I could plunge on with my work,
for I was a writer, and now I had
a fat front desk clerk, a topless bar
next door that pounded disco, new faces
to describe, new lives to invent, yet
another story that wouldn't dent a world
that was sick of stories, but loved them,
so spun them oblivious to weather,
language, logic, or looks.

Writing Class, The Correctional Center

The same night I read yours
about Eddie the Cat Killer,
the friend who caught cats,
burned them, buried the teeth
beneath the high school field's
goal line, I read in the paper
you were sentenced: Thirty years
for killing a nightclub bouncer,
a white man who you said
ogled your white girlfriend,
then came at you with a knife—
so you shot him in the mouth.

When you revise your latest,
tell me about Eddie's grin.
Tell me how he sleeps.

Nine Pieces of Paper

Down to nine pieces of paper, Ken,
a failing village student wrote
late November, then stuck
that message in an envelope,
postage paid by addressee.

Eight days later (a bad storm
had grounded planes), the words
reached me a hundred miles away.
I pictured her, Lois, as I had
six weeks earlier, my visit:

a young, stout, well-meaning woman,
loud, talky, slow, bespectacled,
a mom with twin five-year-old boys,
a four-year-old girl, a husband
away. Where, she didn't know.

A recovering alcoholic, Lois
had escaped that trap
to land in another. Addicted
to bingo, she couldn't keep money,
wouldn't do mental work, lied.

Rereading her note, I wanted
to repeat what I'd told the class
time after time: Call me at home,
at the college, or use the fax.
I wanted to shake that stolid body

with the obvious: Look, Lois,
borrow paper. Or take a dollar
of your bingo money and splurge.
Or at least fill the nine pieces
you do have—yes, both sides.

On a scrap, I scrawled a quick
Keep going, Lois — you can do it,
stuffed it in a mailer with a ream
of blank sheets, And scribbled beneath
the label *Lois, this is your chance.*

Grammar Lesson

I know: Wriggling unconfidently
at desks, my latest freshmen
face the intimacies of script
and space with primal distrust,
as if the type had turned viral
,∴,pqd} 8fu -oo-::oo- boo!

I begin: Grammar's full of pain
because every dot and line
are personal. Like lovemaking.
Like cave paintings. Like breath.
Write for yourself, passionately.
The language will repay you.

Heigh-ho Silver, Away

The work may be daylong sport—
a picnic with a sweetheart
beside a favored waterfall or creek—
or may take weeks in stirrups,
blazing a trail on weary horse
over the sharp-rocked hills
of scrub pine country,
the unflagging quarry
unfazed by wind, rain,
hunger, thirst, the chase
an upward maze, leading
each climb to a new summit
and its gigantic view
of dry sunshine,
or some other mountainous nothing.
Heigh-ho Silver. Ride on,
faithful pony. A northwest peak
shimmers in moonlight.
Poets always get their poems.

Fire Song

This morning, experimenting,
he wrote the words *August Snow*,
and imagined the northwest coast
of Alaska, a white man
looking out a Nome window
at midnight, catching autumn's
first stars over tundra.

This afternoon, experimenting,
he wrote the words *Sister Nightbreak*,
and imagined the convent,
a dry and wrinkly nun asleep
dreaming of crab, salmon, wolf.
He decided her hands were folded
on her belly as if in prayer.

This evening, experimenting,
he wrote the words *Fire Song*,
and imagined a disease burning
itself out. *Take courage*, he wrote,
as if to remind himself
this searching for words
meant long, deep days alone.

The Day After Bukowski Died

Could've gone to the track
won or lost a bundle
on nags that looked hot
in *The Form*.
Could've polished off a six
along the way (listening
to Mahler in the car
on the way home).
Could've sat at the typer
and pounded awhile.
Could've used sex.
Could've if I needed
to pretend
to be somebody I
wasn't. Nope, just went
to the library, handwrote
a little something
in some simple voice
to honor a guy
who'd say any damn thing
on paper and didn't care
what anybody thought
as long as they left him
to enjoy the races,
the beer, the music,
the poems, the women,
left him to live
his crazy, beautiful,
fucked-up life
in peace.

A History of Reading

at two
I read
my first
animal

earlier
I read
the air

in eighth grade
I learned to read
upside-down

after college
I read radio
not revolt

today
I read
inside
an airplane

someday

underground
high schools
will rule
the air

animals
in t-shirts
will rule
the air

revolutionaries
with radios
will rule
the air

we will
all read

flying

Second-Best Friends

I write at night
You write before work
I write in my journal
You write because you need to

We meet and share

You talk about your mother's death
I talk about my new lover
You talk about your dreams
I talk about my father

We return home

I write about your mother's death
You write about my new lover
I write about your dreams
You write about my father

We meet and share

You talk about my father
I talk about your dreams
You talk about my new lover
I talk about your mother's death

We return home

I write about my father
You write about your dreams
I write about my new lover
You write about your mother's death

We meet and share

You talk about your needs
I talk about my journal
You talk about your work
I talk about night

We return home

She Asked Where Poems Come From

Night,
a syllable

lifts
the roof.

Stars
pour in,

followed
by that

marvelous
and witchy

snitch
of moon.

The Substitute Teaches the Sestina

"So, take six words you love.
Any six. Last year a tenth-grader wanted
dead, die, dead, dying, deathwish,
and *suicide*. Her sestina
was an elegy to herself, '*I'm So Dead.*'
Any questions?"

"Yeah, I got some questions.
I don't understand what love's
got to do with being dead.
Also, what if we don't want
to write a sestina.
How about a limerick?" "Yeah, teacher, I wish

we didn't have to write a poem. I wish
I was dead." "Mr. Teacher, my question
is what is a sestina
and how did she fall in love
with one once she wanted
to be dead?"

"Teacher, how can dead
people write?" "Does making a deathwish
count as a poem?" "Why'd you want
to come here and teach?" "I have a question.
Are you married?" "Teacher, I'm in love
with you, and when I grow up I want to be a sestina."

"Yeah, teacher, could you tell us what a sestina
is one more time?" "I know—it's when you're dead
and you write an elegy." "No, it's when you love
six words." "No, it's when you have a deathwish
and you're a poet." "Teacher, I have a question.
To pee or not to pee—do you want

me to pee in my pants?" "Why would anyone want
to pee in their pants?" "Is this a sestina?"
"I haven't been listening. What's the question?"
"Wait. My student began: *Dead, dead, dead, dead,
I'm so dead./ Don't I wish
I could commit suicide./ I'd love*

*to die,/because I want to be dead./
Then, no more sestinas or deathwishes/
or questions about dying,/ or love. . . ."*

Thief
for Sybil Kollar

Call me thief. I steal
from my mother, father, you.
I'm a writer, which is no big deal.

It's not about what I feel,
what I know. Not about where, when, why, who.
Call me thief. I steal

theme, plot, character. I kill,
occasionally, for the exact word. True,
I'm a writer. Which is no big deal.

For I'm a murderer, too, until
I turn it into something new.
Call me thief. I steal

kisses from winter air. I spill
light through sky. I flutter into blue.
I'm a writer. No big deal—

all I do is scribble on the great big wheel
I've borrowed—no, stolen!—from you. You
call me thief. I steal.
I'm a writer. No big deal.

To a Twenty-Year-Old Poet

Forty years old, I'm you times two,
and you think I'm pitiful, a prick,
unknown and unread for good reason
because what I write is "the worst."
Listen, if you're serious about the art,
the usual advice is, first, find something
else to do because poetry is no way
to make a living. Second, read
everything you can, whether you like it
or not. Third, establish a schedule
and write even when you don't want to,
regardless of standards (which doesn't mean
you won't work to make each syllable
sing). Fourth, leave your elders alone,
unless invited, or you risk
being called *asshole* in print. Fifth,
if you haven't quit after ten, fifteen,
twenty years, then write even more,
and — this is important — watch what happens
to you, young man, in the process.

The Lode

So much to do
and I neglect
my outer life
to lie in bed
scribbling lines
that obsess me
for hours, and
the next morning
forget. I can
barely remember
if this is today.

December now,
maybe, and what
can I show for
this long fall
but a great dark
weight of type,
an equivalent
lightening and
quickening within,
the emptying
of deep ore.

Writing Lesson

Though over seventy,
she wore her frizzy purple cap
skull-tight, like a punker's wig.
Nouveau weird/hip and scared
of aging, I decided, watching her
enter the cafe, searching.
I waved her down, Audrey,
my newest student,
beginning writer, long-time
therapist who last week
said over the phone
she hoped her pastiche
of short journal entries
could be shaped into a memoir
"that showed the world
what's what—my story
is central to the era."

Like everyone, I stared
at this jaunty purple-haired
grandmother who was not
purple-haired, not really,
this business relation
I hoped would be easy.

The parts I praised,
she said were no good.
The parts I thought
needed work, she defended
as her very very best.
On and on, this process.
I might have been talking
to my mother, if my mother
had style, and we had
something to talk about.

The Clearest Days

I
When asked what I do,
I answer: poetry.

II
When typing cover letters,
I sometimes write: *Five more —
and thanks for allowing me
to continue this practice.*

III
Having already written,
I walk to the post office,
toss a few new envelopes
with yesterday's rejections
down the mail chute,
then go to my box.
Acceptance or not —
no difference.

IV
An itch turns
into a scratch
turns into a poem.
Any itch. Any
scratch. Any body.

V
When asked what's up,
I unfold my latest, and read.

Fire Starter

Scratch fast, long-hand drafts
on the back of rejected scraps.
Let sit overnight. Dream.
Next day, type to the screen,
print, quit. Hours later,
fidgeting, rereading for rhythm,
pencil in changes so lines
zing. Retype, whistling zippy
fiddle tunes. Double-check
for typos. Shred each sheet
but the last and set with twigs
and sticks in woodstove ash.
Put a match to kindling.
Poke for sparks. Feed wood
until the study is roaring,
the bedroom is toast.

Fiver
   for Phil Dacey

A fiver for Phil
has got to be
a playful page full
of exuberance, a music
you can see, smell,

taste. Music you can
touch. Hear it?
(I'm asking rhetorically —
of course you hear it,
the wee bits

of rhyme, a dark wit
that's quite bright,
an insistent rhythm
that could sit
content at Juilliard.)

A fiver for Phil
could be fingers
crossed in a mitten, a foot
of little curled toes,
change for a ten

with three old ones
and a crisp two dollar bill,
hymns of love
and language, a late
afternoon beer with friends.

Transcendentalist

You browse the poetry daily,
borrow what fits in your pack,
ride a jammed bus home,
skimming stanzas en route.

Months into this, you've built
a house—the accumulated
books and renewals stacked
like bricks around your bed.

Nightly now, in sleep,
you open a window, gaze out
into redeemable and deep
otherwordly truths.

Harvesting the Poetry

Pluck a word and probe gently.
Rub it in your hands. Pick at the stem.
Press the skin, pushing until pressure.
Don't prick. Pluck. Probe gently.

Put several ripening words in a basket.
Position by wine, loaves of bread, a half-full jar,
a window. Play with greens, yellows. Daub orange,
red, pink. Leave the painting for a day,

then add to the table a knife. Such aesthetics—
they'll starve you. Pluck, prick, press,
paint, position, pleasure. You must also quarter,
chew, devour words, swallow the seeds. Lap

the last drop of juice and wipe the sticky dribble
off your chin. Then bite twice, savoring sweet
soft meat in one mouthful, a hard urge for sex
in the other. Afterward belch, realizing, semi-

apologetically, that words lie, that hunger
hurts, that though appetites are insatiable,
we stomach too many flavors, too much
fat to satisfy needs.

Slice this poem into wafer-thin strips
and lay every word in the sun.

When dried to a leathered toughness,
stuff the letters in your pack.

Hike up any mountain trail.
The letters will nourish,

their fuel sustaining
beyond weight.

The Trio

Near Muse

When I am ready,
she decides to take
a walk. When she

is ready, I see
dishes needing doing.
When we are both ready,

Death joins us.

Far Muse

Irked by robins,
herons, lobsters,
frogs, she murmurs

something about
heredity, the cosmos,
those jealous

and artful stars.

Working Muse

Patches, more patches.
Patience, more patience.

He said. She said.

Square by square
we make you this
crazy warm quilt.

The Smaller Journals

One poet chews
   the language a year.

One poet with an ear
   like a colander.

One poet from Kansas
   whose flat voice scratches.

One poet who fancies jazz,
   sex, and matricide.

On and on, these anonymous
   contributors map us.

After Hospice

Metaphor, musicality,
an ecstatic language factory
closes shop after
a half century manufacturing
fine and exact lines that fit

into one another
with a click. Image
and form. A worm
curled at the bottom
of a mezcal bottle,

a brief sermon
would not be unwelcome—
we say it firmly:
nothing is permanent.
It begins with sperm

and an egg. Finally,
we're all terminal.
What's left:
a quickening collage
of light, voice, love,

blues, greens, yellows, reds,
an orange that leaves you
speechless. You remake
yourself into the shade
that's purest poetry.

Your Smarter Self

You want to write a poem.
Okay, find paper and pen.
Transform yourself and become

your smarter self. Go home,
home being the spirit door you must open.
You want to write a poem?

Go back to where you're from,
recall your mother's and father's origins.
Transform yourself and become

mythic midwife, soldier, traveler, bum.
Say you're Midas, Judith, Noah, Aladdin.
You want to write a poem,

so jot, scribble, or type. Find some
words in dreamy darkness. By the end,
transform yourself and become

seer, shaman, jokester, crone,
wolf, owl, turtle, cat. Be a bedouin
if you want. To write a poem,
transform yourself. And become.

Sestina for William Stafford

Of course, the trick to poetry
is to have pen and paper. Words
on a page will make song—
the words can't help themselves. Plain
ones say it better, or so I was taught
by a man born and raised in Kansas,

who took plain Kansas
with him in the poetry
he later wrote. His parents taught
him to honor both land and words.
That wasn't so hard on the plains
where the grass made an easy song

for a boy who listened well, for song
sang everywhere first in Kansas
and then beyond. The plains
later became mountain and coast. Poetry
didn't mind. The words
spilled their magic, taught

him music, taught
him, yes, writing was his song,
that he could scribble gray words,
not just shiny red ones. Kansas
was good enough—and poetry
would nod its head. Simple and plain

it was (though simple and plain
could be profound). Poetry taught
him, too, to question poetry
and reinvent song,
which made for a Kansas
that he filled with words

like *sky, sun, wind*. Words
that started on the plains —
Hutchinson, Kansas —
transported him to Oregon, and taught
him to be. His enduring song:
have pen, paper, and make poetry —

there are only words. He taught
that plain and true made real song.
A Kansas man. His avocation: poetry.

The Leaving

I leave
dead selves in poems.
And I'm relieved

to read what I've cleaved
and burned. Little word-tombs.
I leave

nothing but ash. I give
up ghosts, haunts, sealed rooms.
And I'm relieved—

after all, who grieves
spooks and vacuums.
I leave

that told pain, and weave
new selves in poems.
And I'm relieved

to have survived.
Here, the villanelle home
I leave.
And I'm relieved.

To the Author

Somewhere in the backseat
of every commute between
self-pity and acceptance
sleeps a book of poetry
or prose that dreams

of surprising the driver,
then taking the wheel.
Wake it gently, author,
by jangling the keys.
Slip it that ring for keeps.

23
A Party of Sonnets (Thirty-Four Poems About Writers)

After Hearing John Haines Read

Poet to whom all others are measured
who write of Alaska, he appears tough
as his work, an elemental line, gruff
and lean, an honest being indentured
to land. His speaking voice, long-weathered
by six-month subsistence winters is rough
and smooth at once, as if wide enough
to embrace both poles. Think rock pressured
by ice and light. Think immensities
mated with silence. Think centuries
of fox, bear, marten, beaver, owl. Picture him
silver as snow gathering on birch limb,
gold as some wolves. Or building a fire
in forty below night. Someplace farther.

Upon Rereading Richard Hugo

How strange, I thought, opening to a letter,
a paean to what broke him, that in the midst
of muscle and nerve, to have cracked was
the sure way to force the poet to confer
with madness and self, to seek solace in others,
to heal. Skipping to the dreams, I scanned bits
of rhythm impossible to resist
or translate. The wreckage. Though what better
form to transmit the sense of someone
fallen, the mysterious abyss.
I shut the book, closed my eyes, caught a man
in a kitchen, tossing out good food. His
eyes were red. He'd been sobbing for hours.
His witness: a square gray stone on counter.

Roethke House, After Hours

No mansion, just some small house with a yard
where an unhappy boy dreamed of making
his dark way. I imagined him sleeping:
narrow bed, little room, thin walls, so tired
of the time, his best hours like that, a boy hard
at it, the deep subconscious watering.
Or maybe awake, though lost, a boy waltzing
into yet another book, long journey toward
becoming the learned man who'd read, write,
teach, who'd be so famously difficult
and sick when he wasn't so gentle and fine,
who, yes, would leave this Saginaw behind.
What happened was not his family's fault.
His days were brilliant, sad. Then there was night.

Quintessential Midwest Poet

Might be he on a farm, she in a town,
a cancer doctor in Minnesota,
on the workshop faculty at Iowa,
in awe of cloud, grass, sycamore, the sound
and smell of autumn, how the sun goes down
over a ball field in Indiana,
be part Chippewa, Sioux, Lakota,
Asian, black, gypsy, a juggler, a clown,
an elephant trainer, a Methodist
writing about a fatherly dentist,
or the time a young insurance man sold
himself on a life that got very old.
Likely wise, humble. Distrusts pleasure.
A funny penchant to talk about weather.

Emeritus

Avuncular, Yeatsian, blackbearlike,
the handsome old poet smiled from behind
the lectern, nodded, explained the undefined
spirit breathing beneath a soul. "Psyche
is my all," he chuckled into the mike
between poems. "She's remarkably smart, kind,
deep," then segued into some lines about wind,
a young boy racing downhill on a bike,
a full moon June midnight, air like a fan
powered by dark speed. Clearing his throat twice,
he next read one about his mother's hands,
how she would bathe him as her very Christ.
The poet opened his own palms then—blood—
and smeared his wide forehead, pronounced it good.

Nature Poet

I'd like to typewrite the world as she does:
a canopy of fogbank, cloudswell, mist,
as if the rain had baptized her, and kissed
the hands that tapped the keyboard. A gold buzz
of sun finer than any bee. A fuzz
of moss. A big male mountain like a fist
of granite bulging from the sleeve and wrist
of earth. A gray land that wasn't and was.
She read from memory, face tilted up
transfixed with an absolute exquisite
sublime rapture, as if cocked toward God.
She read like an old owlet, a wolf pup,
like a five foot moth flying into it.
A rare creature caught in the full moon's nod.

Carl Sandburg and His Days

Renaissance man before renaissance man
was a term in vogue. He played music
and wrote poems, of course. His favorite trick
was no trick at all. He was of this land,
of prairie and farm. A curious man,
that meant he took life by steps. He'd stick
himself in Chicago. He worked. He'd stick
himself in North Carolina. His plan
was no plan at all. He did what was needed.
His poems entertained. His poems could feed.
His poems turned to prose. He wrote of Lincoln,
of America, of song. A sly grin.
Poet of the people. Of Illinois.
Sandburg, he was a smart Galesburg boy.

Tropic of Cancer

Brooklyn to Paris to those long Big Sur
years, a classic 20th century
plot, the American writer's journey
to Europe and back. This late-bloomer
wrote as if part of a moving picture,
rolling through book after book, energy
washing glad as a river, the story
how he came to be premier chronicler
of the artist self, sexual being
taking great joy in women, in seeing
all the strange curious ways around him.
That first book was an inky orgasm,
banned for years due to obscenity —
Henry Miller lover of cunt, not country.

Schwartz

Unhappy, so unhappy, precocious
poet and scholar. Delmore. But what could
he have done? He wrote what was so very good
when he was so very young. Atrocious
husband, nomadic professor, ferocious
drunk, difficult friend. Delmore. But what could
he have done? A wretched childhood would
lead him to books. His mind was so precious
when he picked up a pen. He made English
easy and strange, each sentence like a dish
of kosher potatoes or liver. He loved
baseball, alcohol, all the girls above
in the balcony. Delmore. His sad fun
with words bespoke illness. That's what he'd done.

Frost Place

Nothing came easy, but the promises
of such. Maybe next week, next month, next year—
easier times. Maybe tomorrow. Dear
Lord, to be so tested in the business
of living. Lots of babies, the missus
a saint. Lots of teaching jobs, a career
of sorts. Happily, he had an ear
for language and loved the tidiness
of rhyme. He wrote so all could understand,
poems simple and plain as a common man
wearing dark trousers, a white long-sleeved shirt.
He was at home in the trees, fields, weeds, dirt,
and in the ways of an unforgiving,
strict earth. Yes, the harsh business of living.

Each Week From the Prairie
for Mr. Garrison Keillor

Poet of place, though not known for his poems.
They could be sermons, but they're not from church.
He stands onstage, tells long stories that search
for what we hope is true. We listen from
the study, the kitchen, the dining room,
or downstairs in the den. Maybe a birch
is budding, or a blue songbird is perched
on a branch as we look outside, become
lost to it all. Or perhaps we're driving
cross-state to see family, or giving
chase to errands across town, radio
tuned to that deep familiar voice. The show
transports us past Minnesota farmlands
and lakes, delivering us home to friends.

Kerouacian Sonnet

Writer or typewriter? Just burn, burn, burn
so the bebop jazz and everything beat
blast like an old Ford from Larimer Street
to Frisco or New York City, then turn
that jalopy around like a sax. Burn,
burn, burn, more beer, weed, books, then meet
Neal, Allen, Gregory, the boys in heat
to take on the big Buddha world and learn
dharma of mountaintop, sky, desert, road.
Bill Burroughs, Gary Snyder, a whole load
of good men. Mexico City. Lowell, Mass.
The clubs, parties, and girls flew by so fast
it was a dream. Sleep? Stars sparkle brighter
without. Dusk to dawn at the typewriter.

American Dreamer, Hunter S. Thompson

Ah, supreme master gonzo journalist,
you twisted near-fact to new modern kind
of truth. You, good doctor of unhinged mind,
were never merely bugged, but fully pissed,
irked, and provoked. If you didn't exist,
your famed pal, Raoul Duke, might have designed
a worthy duplicate (likely while blind
drunk, and high on acid and speed). A list
of achievements: could outbooze any friend
(gin, vodka, scotch, rum, red wine, beer, bourbon);
inspired countless dumb innocents to aim
for Vegas to scribble dreary and inane
tequila-fueled screeds; coined *Fear and Loathing*,
a stoned take on an empire wearing nothing.

Vonnegut Sonnet

So it goes, the happy darkness—or dark
snap of truth—that ruled him. Husband, father,
writer, veteran, he cut through blather
to bite and make light, to whistle and bark.
He was master eccentric. Kindly shark.
Shrewd purveyor. Clean! (A daily bather.)
Dirty! (There's that mind.) What was the matter
with country, culture, all mankind? He'd park
himself at his desk, recall World War II
and long Dresden nights. Kurt Jr.. Bemused
Indy boy who so fully loved to smoke,
who treated the deep years as fatal joke.
Iconic mustache, untamed hair, a nose
for timeless irreverence. So it goes.

The Wizard

Suspendered, he stepped on stage, smart sharp eyes
scanning the house. *Fine-lookin' crowd*, he crowed,
then stuck a finger in a hardback, bowed,
began to read aloud, voice the rough size
of one of his six foot three, thick-armed, wise-
guy heroes. *Deboree wheelbarrowed a load
of good shit*, he drawled as feedback echoed
through the hall. For two beats he feigned surprise.
And the goddamn mike's full of it, he snorted,
then cracked a joke about choice sixties pranks
and dope, how today got "super-shorted
by Reagan, Bush, and their sleaze-play hijinks."
On and on the writer rollicked. That's Kesey.
Spelled K-E-S-E-Y. Real life poetry.

Native Writer

If I closed my eyes, the voice might have been
Silko, Harjo, Alexie spinning tales
within tales of what it means to inhale
and exhale as the true American
Indian: a breathy desperate grin
and chuckle that hammers seven-inch nails
of spirit into earth. But since voice fails
to tell all, I looked, took the round face in,
caught sparkling light across glasses, and flashed
on the students to whom I grew attached
in Nome. Folks with names like Ongtawasruk,
Saccheus, Tocktoo, Olanna, Okpealuk.
Journal entries about whale meat, wolf ruff,
walrus hunts. Typical Bering Straits stuff.

Minimalist, Perhaps

Take a shy boy. Give him books, paper, pens.
Take him fishing. Give him beer, some drinks,
a young girlfriend he gets pregnant. He thinks
it will all be good. He writes stories, sends
them out, gets a few published. Two children
have needs. So does the wife. Years pass. He blinks
at the face in the mirror, pours a drink,
then one more. How did this ever happen?
The drinking. It gets so very messy
until he quits. It's either that or die.
His work is spare—quiet epiphanies,
maybe—marked by plain talk, love, sadness, lies.
The damage? Just say it was a lot.
Remarried, buoyant, he never forgot.

For a Difficult Teacher
in memory of Wendy Bishop

Her eyes a photographer's eyes—clear, sharp,
hard as raw light. Her manner even
sharper, though tempered now and again
by wry music from an interior harp,
a wit that chimed. Steely resolve. A warp
for work. I thought us good, casual friends
because we shared school gossip, a passion
for getting things done. Oh god how we carped
about this or that campus absurdity—
until I took a graduate class from her.
Stubborn me. Stubborn and difficult her.
Because she could, she smacked me with a B.
Wendy Wendy, she was such a stickler
for process. I wrote too damn quick for her.

Bard of the Aleutians
in memory of Jerah Chadwick

Friends, if we can sing it, we don't want it,
he crooned, making lit journal slush an event.
Three decades later, I still picture him bent
at desk, grad student star, teacher, poet,
Permafrost co-editor. His sly wit
supported me in my own first attempts
at verse—how he made me laugh. Three years went—
he returned to the Aleutians. I graduated
Fairbanks too, moved to Juneau, Sitka, Nome,
and beyond. Our far-flung paths crossed a few
times more—readings or parties here and there
Did I ever formally thank him? Each poem
I published I owed him. He wrote so true,
pure. Like his gusty Unalaska air.

Poetry Reading, Fairbanks

I slipped in late, caught the last few poems
of some unsung local speaking before
a dozen folks. Or maybe a few more.
And attentive—I could hear the *hmmmmmms*
and *ahhhhhs*, laughter at the right spots. The poems
hammered like consecutive knocks on a door.
Or a big engine about to turn. Or
a house being labored into home.
As if each intended syllable framed
a foundation of muscle and toil, the dark
basement soil of communal memory.
The poet? No book, no following, no name—
just someone sharing original work.
Formally informal. Spirited. Free.

Open Mike

Trite rhymers, drunk potheads, anguished lovelorn
hipster ain'ts, misunderstood songster-punks
parade onstage, mainly to posture and clunk
and salute one another, recite porn
odes and neo-beat pleas to be reborn
as priestess, as rock star, as clown, as hunk,
the false gems of images like the junk
and clang of TV. I don't know. I'm torn
between a chaotic democracy
that allows each and every poet a chance
to speak as equals, and a philosophy
of "them that got two left feet shouldn't dance
with yours truly." I arrive late, leave early,
recall my youthful work, which was lousy.

Journeyman

Author of five critically well-received
barely-read books, he makes decent money
as writer-in-residence at "this funny
two-bit piece-of-shit school you can't believe—
so I wrote it." His new novel, conceived
as satire, includes a teacher, Sonny,
who, in his own words is "a stud honey
of a pig, a man mighty greatly relieved
to be divorced, except for that simple
matter of a thing named alimony."
Sonny, like his creator, has wide dimples,
a fearsome reaction to matrimony,
supplements his income with short reading tours—
getting paid, in part, by bedding juniors.

Best-Seller

Widely known for writing the zipless fuck—
since then a long, notorious career
colored by that phrase. She swears critics leer
no matter what, because it's zipless fuck
here, zipless fuck there, that infamous fuck
all hers forever to those puerile ears.
Onstage, she's brassy, bemused, all good cheer
and smarts, making light of the zipless fuck
because this is a curious country,
seven parts puritan to one part lewd,
where people marry, divorce, get stuck—
so what, we're impassioned souls so hungry,
so driven, so tight, who screw and get screwed,
fuck and get fucked (zippered or zipless fuck).

The Suicide

You had it all almost, didn't you: friends
who loved and admired you, the accolades
of colleagues who mattered, a job that paid
well at a small Southern college that tended
to the absolute brightest. Who knew when
you went stranger, became star that faded
in the vast and complicated night, made
the descent from genius to how it ended
with a rope around your neck, your feisty wife
to find you hanging your ironic life.
What was the secret that tortured you so?
A story: You were sick, getting sicker.
Your wife was tired. So were you. You said no
more fighting pain. Pills were slow. Death, quicker.

Hemingway Spots Faulkner in a Bar

I walk in, size the postman up. That's what
men do. We eat, drink, hunt, fight. We read.
We write for our lives so the pages bleed
stories. I go in with a long knife, cut
the fat. All red meat. Rich. The sweetest nut.
Love, loss, hunger, ambition, weakness, greed.
I cross lands, seas, skies, taking as I need
to pin down readers, punch them in the gut.
I admit the fisherman vexes me,
his mean ego, an insecurity
that diminishes an aptness that ought
to have done more, though that's fancy half-thought,
my sense. So I nod to the fellow scribe,
catch his eye, raise a glass — cross-room we imbibe.

First Novelist

Sad-looking Mississippian begins
with the family tree, ends with a prayer,
in between reads, softly, a most bizarre
Gothic tale: a pair of identical twins
are separated at birth. One named Vin
at age twenty has a sex change, becomes Claire,
moves to New Orleans, falls in love with Bear,
who—you've guessed!—is his/her brother. Within
the first ten pages all this plus a murder/
suicide in some club. The French Quarter
has never seen such a stew. Further
twists include a ménage à trois with Carter,
Vin/Claire and Bear's crazy dwarf whore mom, who
recognizing her kids, goes mad anew . . .

Another Generation

I saw the queer horny poet and beat
once in Cambridge where he crooned the blues,
next at Duke where he made the evening news
for urging male profs to unsheathe cocks and meet
with the students, next in a dark backstreet
dream where he appeared as the bearded muse
grandfather who raped me—calling me his deuce
while licking off his come, then kissing my feet.
Ambitious prick, he's worked overtime as
corrupter and taboo-buster, bop jazz
bard, howling asshole, placid saint, public
bosom pal and defender of Jack,
embodiment of all things Whitmanesque,
king fool Buddhist Jewboy of zen burlesque.

Ghostwriter

At first I thought it strange that a black man
rose to talk about his role as ghost.
I'd imagined writerly ghosts to be lost
scared white guys, thin and pale with trembly hands,
not this rugged broad-shouldered African
giant who looked like he played low post
for the Knicks. A tower almost. A boast
of a man. A swagger. A guy bigger than
his celebrity author's accomplishment.
Why did he, I wondered, choose to write
without a single public acknowledgment
in return. The business transformed insight
to a shell game. Then the ghost touched his heart,
and claimed Ralph Ellison had cast the part.

Re-Joyce: A Portrait

Musician, his preferred chord was the word
on page. From poem to short story to song,
a blind rhapsody so complex and long
to be part orchestral chant, part absurd
sound installation—narrative deferred—
he let eye-full visions lead him along
this novel path and that. Pleasure's not wrong,
the master at play, adding a small bird,
a hound, foxes, a manor, a lady,
or else nothing of the sort, a jumble
of syllables and noise to make intense
lazy summer days, a big oak shady
and sad, a young boy taking a tumble
from branch, music the journey to silence.

For James Tate

Take flight. Throw a horseshoe. It might grow wings
and aim for clouds. If it hits just right, sun-
light will make halos for every citizen
angel. Otherwise, rain, and what rain brings.
A small boy may cry. Ballgame postponed. Things
go wrong. He thinks life is all about fun—
bright days of play and love. That quick it's done:
twenty-four hours, then weeks, months, years, the rings
of the oak, holding onto its secret—
it, too, flies when the old roots say enough.
What is the world but a cycle of dreams:
we take off again, again. Each little bit
a birth and a death. How can we not laugh
at the sad beauty. Nothing is what it seems.

The Good Doctor

Plums? What better fruit to explain a mood,
to balance the long day's diagnoses
and healings. He tended them all—bum knees,
sore throats, rashes, infected cuts, births—would
listen close. Quintessential neighborhood
physician, stethoscope and bag, disease
whisperer whose manner put fears at ease.
He prescribed when to eat and sleep, what should
happen after a course of medicine.
Life in Rutherford, so near Paterson
and New York City. He'd sit at desk, write
the difficult news. Content, but not quite.
People suffered, died. Children, too. Later,
for small pleasure, to the refrigerator.

Travel Writer

Muse for Timbuktu, Istanbul, Tangiers,
and the rest, she pens jittery memoirs
fueled by caffeine. All question-and-answer,
her recent talk ranged from the best pub beer
in Ireland and Wales, to why one should steer
clear of Hong Kong, to exactly how far's
the trip from Casablanca to Dakar,
to what's been her closest calls, her worst fears.
Ten years on the road, she's like to settle
but can't because of this funny little
bug that keeps her on the move, taking notes
and photos. Rapid voice, pretty face, she totes
her own around the globe. Best place on earth,
someone asks. She replies: a quiet berth.

Homesteader
  — in memory of John Haines

That winter night I was in Seattle
when a Fairbanks friend sent a brief note
with a link, then added a John Haines quote.
In a blink—and Haines might have named his full
sum of days as no more than that—the call
to live morally each hour, to never doubt
the stars, to plant acres of potatoes and oats.
Nature, he might well have said, is final
arbiter, and we're here on earth to serve.
March 2, when my friend wrote, was the fifteenth
anniversary of my plane crash near Nome.
How our lives unfurl as crookedy curve.
You and I can now point to the zenith.
John Haines has found his ultimate home.

Bill Stafford, 100

Bill Stafford would never claim perfection,
the neat round number. Rather, he was about
edges, observation, lingering doubt,
the stuff of happenstance and reflection,
ease and mystery. He'd ask sly questions,
answer with a slight shrug or nod. No shouts.
Lines might include mountain, wind, button, trout,
family. He was without pretension.
If he were still alive at one hundred,
I'd guess him still alert, sturdy enough
to jot a few dozen early morning words.
To acknowledge the day, he might have said,
For the sky, a century's not so tough.
Then he'd take pen, write of cloud, weather, bird.

24
How I Make a Living in Poetry
(A Review and Summary)

Every so often someone will come up and tell me I'm one of the rare poets who makes a living from their poetry.

It's not exactly like that, I'll say, and explain that though I have the credentials to legitimately call myself "a poet," poetry alone isn't what's getting me paid. I find work because I also play fiddle, and have found a way to incorporate poetry with music. Because I've already been doing this for years, I not only have a network of contacts, but the wherewithal to use them. I earn a reasonable income doing work I love.

In 1988 I graduated from University of Alaska Fairbanks with an MFA in Creative Writing, an emphasis in fiction writing. After teaching full-time for several years, since 1995 I've been a freelance writer, musician, performer, and educator. When pressed for a more specific description of my job, I'll say I'm a touring artist (though for many years I'd have answered *Alaska's Fiddling Poet*; the moniker has both drawbacks and benefits—and I'll still use it when it can help secure a date).

The vast majority of my income stems from appearances, and I play a range of venues for a range of audiences. In the course of a week I might entertain an auditorium of first-graders, fourth-graders, or middle-schoolers, work with at-risk or AP high-schoolers, visit a college creative writing classroom, do a solo show at a public library, participate in and produce a roots music variety show through an arts council or performing arts center.

Despite the differences in venue and audience, the one constant is that I'll combine poetry with music and storytelling.

At most events—and certainly all my school shows save for the largest assemblies—I make time for a question-and-answer session. If the question comes up, I'll mention to high school or middle school groups that I'm being paid to be at their school. What I don't explain is how I've found a way to successfully do this.

The money hasn't come from selling books. Though my first two full-length collections both went into second printings, most of the proceeds went to the publisher and distributor. My next four collections have sold well enough, as have my memoir and my children's book of acrostic poems. But from the beginning—and my first full-length collection came out in 2000—what's felt essential has been making sure books, which I've had to buy from various publishers, have gotten into the hands of people with budgets who might hire me.

In other words, because I make money from appearances, I strategically give away books because it's having written books, rarely the actual writing, that gets me hired.

It's one thing to do a reading in a bookstore, and hope to sell books. It's another thing to do a reading and visit classes at a university, hope to sell books, and be paid an honorarium. And it's yet another thing to be hired by an arts council or performing arts center to do a public show, offer community outreach, hope to sell books, and fulfill a contract where the guaranteed pay usually far exceeds what a university English Department offers.

My CDs, which combine poetry with Appalachian-style string-band music, have always sold better than the books. But even these disks, combined with sales of the books, usually only bring in enough to pay for incidentals.

My long-time challenge has been to keep booking appearances that not only pay well enough to enable me to make rent, buy food, and transport myself around the country, but also to re-order the books and CDs. If I don't invest in the process, I'd have to quit. While the poetry and music are available online—and my website has evolved to better document the work—it makes a difference when I can get the books and CDs in people's hands.

Once hired, I trust I'll do a good enough job that I'll be rehired in the next year or two, or that my contact at the organization will pass my name to a colleague.

Ultimately, I'm a businessperson working a job.

Or, better, a *small* businessperson working a job that includes sharing poetry with people, most of whom are unfamiliar with contemporary poetry.

I've just described the bare bones of the real work, which is the hustle for gigs. The fun part is going somewhere and making art come alive. Here, I recall Emily Dickinson's dictum: "If I feel physically as if the top of my head were taken off, I know *that* is poetry."

So that's the aim: taking off the top of people's heads. If I'm going to spend my life playing music and reading poems in front of people, I better have something especially worthwhile to offer.

Visiting a graduate school program or a writers' conference, I might explain how one of my graduate school professors tried to dissuade me from writing poems—after all, I'd entered my program as fiction writer and graduated with a fiction writing emphasis—yet learned enough from that professor to write poems for class which were among the first I later had published.

I'll share some of those early poems as well as poems about teaching writing, poems which don't resonate in all settings, but do amidst writers. Other poets may insist that it's the responsibility of an audience to follow where the poet wants to take them, no matter the difficulty and the challenges, and that, indeed, it's every poet's responsibility to stretch audiences in various ways.

It's these other poets' right to think that. But that's a luxury I don't have.

Because my livelihood depends on connecting with an audience, I choose poems, tunes, and stories that take that into account. If I lose an audience, especially a younger one, even for a few minutes, I might not get it back. But if my visit induces a single attendee to rehink his or her relationship with language and the world, I've succeeded. Of course, I want to influence them all.

The question then becomes how to give an audience compelling enough poems. Since I know nothing about any particular group except where they live and, sometimes, the organization they're affiliated with, I use those clues as my guide. But, again, how can I induce a general audience in a theater to pay attention? How do I engage hundreds of elementary school or middle school students sitting in a gym or a cafeteria?

The answer: I'm always going to share poems where there's the best chance of establishing an authentic exchange between myself and my audience. The poems themselves will necessarily vary by setting. If I already have poems that best fit the occasion, great, If not, I get to work writing them.

It helps, too, to mix the delivery of poems: some I'll read from a book or sheet of paper; others I recite from memory (read your own strong, reliable poems often enough and you, too, will commit them to memory); others I introduce by telling a story. Because I play fiddle, I've learned to separate spoken word by fiddle interludes. It's like serving crackers during a wine-tasting. I've also taken the step of making the music an integral part of those poems and stories.

For instance, when doing shows for a general audience, I'll often bring an accompanist who plays fiddle or banjo and share poems about the music. When I read to actual live fiddle or banjo music, then pick up my fiddle myself, the reading has reached another level. Performance? Sure. Why not?

Not a musician yourself? What's stopping any of us, I wonder, from writing a poem, or a sequence of poems, based on a favorite song or musician? What's stopping us from writing poems that can be arranged for music, or enhanced by music, and then bringing along a musician to a reading? If each poem in a successful collection is to stand alone, and the full collection is to function as one exceptionally long poem, why not aspire to to the same standard when it comes to readings. Why not choose poems that purposefully make better theater?

Anybody writing ekphrastic poems can show the pieces of art that inspired the poems being read — with extra points to the writer who's also the visual artist.

What's stopping any of us from writing poems that more directly engage a particular audience?

For young audiences, my work has evolved so I now write an age-appropriate poem for every school or community I visit. As the visiting (paid) writer — perhaps the only "poet" these students will ever meet — that's become an essential part of the day's work: I'll not only write something original for the place, but will type, print, cut, and hand out poems to every student, along with one of my poetry bookmarks.

September 2014, when I visited three high schools in Caldwell County, North Carolina, each student received a bookmark, and a small sheet with the following two poems:

A Caldwell County Poem

Cheeseburgers, chocolate,
and coffee. Begin in
Lenoir, leave for Asheville,
Durham, Charlotte, Boone,
way down to Atlanta even.
Everywhere is home. You can't
lose it, really. You'll never
lose it, the place you grew up.

Cured tobacco or ham, church
on Sunday or Wednesday, calculus,
uncles, aunts, cousins. Maybe you'll
never leave this place in the hills.
That's okay, too. Either way,
you know where you're from.

A Special Caldwell County Poem

Call it your life. Make magic
as you go. Magic? Carolina
lets you have these crazy fall
days, both happy and sad.
What? Some of what I know:
Earth can be a weird place.
Last night there was road kill.
Love can push; love can pull.

Call it your life. Make magic
or make a promise as you go.
Understand? Yes? No? Do you?
Next week is not the plan.
The time is now. This is it.
Your magic life. Work & play.

November 2013, I wrote these two for at-risk middle-schoolers at the Lincoln School in Kokomo, Indiana:

A Lincoln Poem

Lots of things happen
in this school. I know that.
No, I don't know details.
Consider this. If I just
observe, I'll not only
learn, I'll be inspired.
Next, I might even write.

A Special Lincoln Poem

Let me explain the usual.
I write different poems. I
notice everything I can
Can you do this magic?
Of course. It's easy to
let your mind fully sail.
Notice everything you can.

Spring 2012, I wrote these for first- and second-graders at Bellamy Elementary in Tampa, Florida, where the school's mascot is a bobcat:

A Bellamy Poem

Boys and girls sit in
every class. Some
love reading. Some love
lunch. Some love
art and music. Some love
math. Some love poems.
You, what do you love?

A Special Bellamy Poem

Be a bobcat. Don't be a crab.
Eat a great big juicy orange,
lots of vegetables too. We'll
look out the windows. Will
an animal walk by? Florida
makes me happy. Yes, I'm
your poetry friend today.

Most kids everywhere have seen acrostics, even if they don't know the name of the form. But few have seen them with line breaks, and fewer still (approximately the same number of high-schoolers that have encountered sestinas or villanelles) have come across double acrostics, where the same word is spelled with both the first and last letters of each line. I title the poems simply, which lets students know the poem is of their place. The title also spells the acrostic.

Even high-schoolers will ooh and ahh upon finding the acrostics—if someone in the group doesn't discover them on his or her own, even after my clues, I'll explain the trick. Getting such a reaction, which usually sweeps the room in a wave, I know my work has value. Emily Dickinson, I think, would approve.

When I see students try their own acrostics, or start writing enthusiastically from another of my prompts, I know I've earned my fee. Walt Whitman, I think, would be proud.

When I later receive students' letters or poems in the postal mail, I'm delighted to have been of service. I make copies of these to pass along to the sponsors of my visit.

This process is one more way for writers to get by in the world.

More than that, this is about poetry, music, art, education, hope.

It's the belief that every occasion has possibilities.

25
Three Essays

I couldn't not include these three essays, which explain how I've gone about writing and publishing the series of books about Donald Trump.

The Gray Area

I recently read that a well-known press was fast-tracking three Donald Trump-inspired books for a May 2017 release, each with 25,000-copy print runs. The idea was to take full advantage of the public's fascination with the Trump presidency.

Interesting, I thought, that this was considered newsworthy. I'm writing this in late February 2017, and six weeks earlier I'd had delivered 400 copies of a full-length poetry collection, *Trump Sonnets, Volume 1*. 75 of those were now in the Berkeley, California warehouse of Small Press Distribution, ready to be sent where ordered. The book's official March 1 release date was in less than a week, and the publisher and I only had 60 books left from that initial run. Back in mid-January, we'd ordered another 1,000 copies, which had just been shipped. Some would go directly to my publisher. Most were due to arrive at my home office in Louisiana either today or tomorrow.

I don't know what's smaller here: my reputation, or my publisher's. We both have little presence in this industry. Yet there are advantages with being small; this timely book couldn't have come out this soon if we were bigger. Including what's at the distributor's, and taking into account the 40 extra books we had to special order late January—I'll explain this later—so far we've moved almost 380 copies. Some were for review. Some were comp copies. Some were part of a two-for-one campaign I started when hand-selling the book. Already we've almost broken even, which feels gratifying.

The story of this book begins with my incredulity that Donald Trump was chosen 45th president of the United States; I'd thought his background and campaign activities made him unelectable.

Wednesday, November 9, I was set to begin nine days in Bowling Green, Kentucky, doing a handful of public events as well as visiting local and regional schools. Amid that busyness, I reflected how Donald Trump made 43rd U.S. president, George W. Bush, seem like a statesman. I scribbled a few words about that, and the next day made a sonnet.

Two weeks later, done with the Kentucky job, I wrote another sonnet about Donald Trump, whose actions and pronouncements carried additional weight now that he was president-elect. For many years now, writing poems had been one of my ways to process difficult or disturbing times.

The week after Thanksgiving, I flew to Buenos Aires to visit a friend whose studio living space had no internet connection. She liked to sleep in. So each morning, before she awoke, I'd sit at a table, and draft three or four new sonnets. I sometimes had a knack for writing quickly and found a groove there in Argentina. After waking, my friend laughed watching me count syllables with my fingers, but that was part of the sonnet-writing. Some of these new poems were in the voice of the president-elect;

others I addressed to him.

I left Buenos Aires after nine days with more than thirty poems. They seemed good enough, I thought, which meant I had, perhaps, half of a book. If I could write two more sonnets a day for the next fifteen days, I'd have a full-length collection. Propelled by momentum — and daily news stories — the next week I wrote twenty more. At that point, I began planning.

First, I phoned a friend who had a background in small press publishing. He volunteered to format everything but the cover, so at some point I could send to a printer a PDF file that conformed to industry standards.

Next, I called the publisher who had released my most recent book, one much like this. If I needed to, I'd publish this myself, but with a publisher there would be greater opportunity for review, and the book would qualify for prizes and awards. Because timing felt critical here, what was most important was speed. Having once self-published a book that a publisher had decided not to reprint a second time, and having also self-published a children's book, I had ISBN numbers handy. I knew I could do this wholly on my own, though hoped I wouldn't have to.

I read him a Trump sonnet over the phone and that quickly I had a publisher for the project. However, it was understood that though he'd be supplying the Ridgeway Press name and ISBN number — and, now that he had national distribution, an established channel for getting the book to the world — I'd be taking care of the book design and the printing, and the financial risk. That was fine with me; if self-publishing, I'd be doing all this anyway. Plus in the long run I knew from experience it was much more economical for me to pay for printing than to pay the publisher for copies.

Next on the list was assembling material for the back cover. I solicited one writer for an endorsement, and asked another for permission to excerpt lines from a book review. Fully aware that what could most distinguish this book was a speedy path to publication, I briskly revised poems (even as I continued to write new ones), gave them titles—none had titles at that point!—fixed typos, ordered them, and composed an acknowledgment page and a table of contents. On December 26, I emailed this document as an attachment to the friend who was going to format the collection. I copied both the publisher, and the endorser-to-be.

For the front cover, I made a rough mock-up of an idea I had, and hoped it would help whoever finally took over that task.

Three days later, December 29, I was leaving my base in Louisiana to go on tour. Because my upcoming schedule included this year's February 8-11 AWP Conference in Washington DC—the perfect place for a book launch—we now had a deadline. However, not only was I about to drive to a job in North Carolina, but from January 5-10 I was going to participate in and produce two big shows in conjunction with an arts conference in New York City. From there, I'd be working two jobs in upstate New York, two more in Michigan, and then would be attending a conference in Madison, Wisconsin. Next, I had several early February jobs in New Jersey and Virginia prior to the DC conference.

Though I had this schedule, I had no idea where I'd be staying most nights, which made planning for book delivery daunting. Another factor was the cost of manufacturing and marketing books. This publisher could only help a little with this. My own budget was limited because I'd spent money on other things: a month earlier this project hadn't even been imagined.

I set off from Louisiana confident that my designer would complete his tasks, that my publisher would send me the ISBN information I'd requested, and that the writer whom I asked for an endorsement would comment positively. I'd already received permission to quote from the reviewer who'd liked my prior book, so at least that was done.

The prior week I'd also started researching print shops. Did I want to follow up with a New Jersey company, which would allow me to pick up the books when I'd be working nearby in early February? Or did I want to go with the Ohio shop that offered what seemed an astounding two-day turn-around on more expensive, but still reasonably-priced, printing? The latter company, for an additional fee, offered a range of cover templates, and could sell me a bar code for my back cover. I researched one more spot, a Michigan-based printer. The company's quote was much cheaper than both the Ohio and the New Jersey companies, but it could only promise a four-to-five-week delivery. That timeline didn't even guarantee I'd have the books for the Washington DC conference.

Driving north, I kept turning over options. While the Ohio print shop might have templates for various front covers, I still needed images for most of the choices. I wondered whether I should pay for rights to some kind of already published image, or come up with something wholly original and properly pay a designer?

New Year's Eve, en route to the performance, my car started making noises. I was able to get to the show with my accompanist, but had to buy a set of tires and get the car re-aligned. There went my coming month's financial cushion. Arriving in New York City on Tuesday, January 3, I decided on the Ohio print shop. It wasn't the absolute cheapest alternative, but if I could have the books proofed by Friday, which seemed probable, they'd be printed Monday and Tuesday, shipped on Wednesday, and would arrive in Detroit where my accompanist lived, and where we were going. That meant I'd have the books for two Michigan events that weekend and for the conference in Madison the following week, when Donald Trump was to be inaugurated. The timing felt right and if I sold a few books, it would justify spending the extra money.

By mid afternoon, January 4, the publisher had not yet passed along an ISBN number. Without it, I'd either have to keep waiting, or use one of my own numbers to self-publish. At that point I also decided to jettison the design I'd envisioned, and settled on a template that featured a simple text-only front cover.

Most everything was falling into place. If the endorser couldn't get to it, we had a back cover with the reviewer quote and a short bio. My accompanist had read the manuscript, and found a handful of errors. My designer had also pointed out typos. After making corrections, I went through the manuscript yet again, confident it was clean. Once we had an ISBN, we could finalize things. Self-publishing wasn't ideal, but I was prepared to move as necessary.

Wednesday evening, January 4, the publisher emailed me an ISBN; I forwarded the number to the designer, who added it to the copyright page. Thursday morning, January 5, I paid for a 400-copy print run, sent a PDF of the inside text, and gave the in-house designer the necessary information for the front and back cover. That afternoon I received the proofs. After my show that night, I made a few small changes to the back cover, then re-sent the file. The next day, Friday, January 6, I was sent a new proof, which I quickly approved. Six days later, Thursday, January 12, three boxes awaited me in Detroit.

I sold books at events in Detroit and Midland, more at the conference in Madison. Though the first 400 copies would get me through the coming month, I had a three-month tour in March, April, May. If the four-to-five week turn-around that Michigan printer quoted was accurate, I could order 1,000 more books. Most would be shipped to Louisiana, the rest to the publisher. We'd need more, especially since we had to send 80 books to the distributor, and at least 25 for review. I was short on money, but having just worked a handful of jobs I had enough to go ahead with the order.

A week later, proofing this new edition, I found a small typo on the back cover as well as a bigger typo within one of the poems. Fixing the typo inside the manuscript was quick, easy, and only cost $10. Correcting the typo on the back cover came with a $160 fee. While there must have been a way to have someone cheaply turn that mistyped period into a comma, I realized I'd either have to begin from scratch, or live with the error. Or else I could order more books with the 2-day turn-around so the designer there could make the easy correction within the project file. I chose the latter option, and ordered 40 more books at $5 each, a relatively expensive short run. The books arrived safely the next week where I was working in New Jersey, and I used them, with the now typo-free back cover, as review copies. More importantly, the quick fix meant we could stay on schedule. I only had a two-week window in late February when those thousand books could safely be delivered to a place I could easily store them.

Trump Sonnets, Volume 1 is my seventh poetry collection. It's the second time I've done a poetry collection mostly myself, but under the auspices of a known publisher. Admittedly, it's a gray area. Who wouldn't want the name of Norton, or University of Pittsburgh, or Copper Canyon on a poetry collection, along with the accompanying marketing and support? No publisher is going to be perfect, but the more-established and respected presses have their resources, and their reputations can certainly help for grants, awards, and fellowships.

But working with one of those presses can take years from initial query to actual publication. Unless already a very big name, the only way to get something out as quickly as we've just done with *Trump Sonnets, Volume 1*, is to do it yourself, or find a publisher motivated to drop everything to work on your behalf. Or to do as I've just done: find a publisher who'll offer you an opportunity to do it yourself.

Having the national distribution that Ridgeway Press enjoys means any bookstore can order the book, and it's available through Amazon. I couldn't have done that by myself. And while there's never going to be a guarantee for a grant, award, or fellowship, at least I can apply for prizes that are unavailable for self-published work.

A month ago, I left a copy of the book in an iconic East Coast bookstore, followed up with an email to the book buyer, who two weeks ago responded that while many patrons shared the sentiment included in my book, there simply was not enough space in the store for this.

In other words, he didn't think the book was good enough.

About the time I got that response, I'd just stopped in another independent bookstore, this one in a large Midwest city. There, the two owners bought 25 directly from me, and wrote me a check.

In other words, they thought the book was good enough.

I recently spoke with a publicist who advised me that I'd be wasting my money paying someone to help with this. Poetry is too hard a sell, the publicist said. Actually, all books are a hard sell right now, she continued.

But it's about Donald Trump, I said, and pointed to the book which I'd set on the table, *Trump Sonnets, Volume 1*, the title emblazoned on a front cover the color of orange sherbet.

She sighed.

I took her advice that I'd be better served continuing to market it myself. Some places, I just sent the book and one-sheet for review. Others, I briefly queried by email, asking if there was interest in a review copy. And others I sent a quick email to say I'd already sent a copy so please be on the look-out. The same short query that elicited virtually no response from most reviewers, received a rapid reply from a major newspaper editor, asking that a second copy be sent directly to a home address.

In other words, whether big or small, whether black or white or gray, sometimes there's rejection, sometimes acceptance. Tastes vary in any business, and this is certainly a business. The only thing we can control is the actual writing. And if the quality is high enough and if we keep doing the best we can, at least we have a chance.

The other day at a large gathering I showed the new book to a friend, and made one of my two-for-one pre-publication $15 sales. A few minutes later, I was approached by someone I didn't know, who simply said that I had a book he wanted to buy, and gave me a twenty. I went into my daypack, pulled out two books, one for him, one for him to pass along. It's two-for-one, I explained. He happily took the second book, and waved off the $5 change.

Having a stranger show interest in something we've written, isn't that part of why we all do this?

If I had been adamant about having these poems published more traditionally, I'd still be waiting for the tangible book, even if it had been accepted instantly when I could have first sent it out right after Christmas. If I'd done it wholly myself, I'd have a book no one could buy unless they saw me in person, or came upon my website, or discovered me through social media (a forum I prefer not to patronize—the subject of another essay).

We're always better served by finding a way through that is in synch with our nature.

I take solace that I've found a process that works for me. Today, I'm almost a dozen poems into *Trump Sonnets, Volume 2*.

He's not changing; for now, neither am I.

Donald Trump is My Muse

Tuesday, August 8, 2017, and I'm working with my publisher to get a manuscript to the printer in Ohio that turns books around in two days. We don't have a publicist. Or, rather, I'm the publicist, just like I was for the two prior books we've done. That's a trade-off of working with a small press. One big advantage is we can get a timely book out quickly. But our budget is minuscule. And for this book there's just me and the publisher, who occasionally does this amid his many other projects.

Our plan is to get me books by Friday, August 18. With an official January 2018 publication date, that would give me a week to properly send out the book for review. Thursday evening, August 24, I'm to leave from near Lafayette, Louisiana for an eleven-week tour, first stop a 1,000-mile drive to a conference that begins Monday, August 28 in Columbus, Ohio. From there I drive 2,500 miles to Seattle for another conference, then jobs in Oregon, California, Nevada, back to Washington state, and Montana. On the road, it's so much tougher to mail packets like this—and if you're reading this after receiving the packet, you have an idea why. This new book is titled *Trump Sonnets, Volume 2*, and in many packets I've also stuffed *Trump Sonnets, Volume 1*, which was published six months ago.

That earlier book got in our hands the second week of January. Because the publisher was busy with other commitments and I was on tour, we couldn't even get review copies out until mid-February, just weeks before the official release. Though having the book by mid-January ultimately proved smart—at a range of events in a range of places, I'd never before had such an easy book to sell—we didn't do as well with reviews. It was a challenge to even land the eight bookstore gigs we did confirm those next months. I vowed to do my next book differently.

For this, then, I found distinctive envelopes, stuck in both of the Trump collections, plus material that was part of the big mailing I recently completed for the performing arts market. I also included the national review we did receive for *Trump Sonnets, Volume 1* along with the *Austin Chronicle* preview of my July bookstore appearance, where the weekly ran my photograph and listed me as one of the week's entertainment picks.

I also decided to include this essay, which first I had to write.

It's another of the joys, and perils, of small-press publishing. When the publisher, or the author, has an idea, there's nothing stopping them but the limits of their resources.

Donald Trump is My Muse

Donald Trump, it's now nine months since you've been
elected U.S. President. Crazy,
isn't it, how you've embraced such lazy,
destructive policy, become champion
villain and freak. You embody the sins
of our age. Nine months! This is your baby,
making daily drama instead of safely
guiding a diverse, powerful nation.
This, the hundred and fortieth sonnet
I've written about you these nine months, means
I've taken you in as I would lover.
I can't stop. I won't stop. I'm in on it,
our public obsession. You're the obscene
secret. I'm the poet discoverer.

There, and I count the 71 sonnets in the first collection, the 68 in the second, and now this, written today, all in the 39 weeks since the election. That's an average of three and a half poems a week, or one every other day.

Donald Trump must be my muse, all right. What the hell happened? And what does that even mean?

Before the 2016 presidential election, I'd read enough about Trump to feel concern as the polls tightened. The last week of October, when one outlet claimed Trump had a 10-15% chance of winning, I grew alarmed. 10-15%? From what I knew of him from the past months of casual reading, his chances should have been zero.

I spent part of Election Day at a meeting in Nashville, then drove to Bowling Green, Kentucky, where I had more meetings scheduled on Wednesday before beginning a nine-day arts and education residency there on Thursday. I watched the election returns in a lonely motel room, and went to bed dispirited. Wednesday morning, listening to the radio in the car before heading to my first appointment, I found a pen and notepad, and wrote, "You make George W. seem a statesman, your opening trick," a sentence which became the first line and a half of a sonnet I finished a few days later.

I wrote two more Donald Trump-inspired sonnets over the next weeks, then flew to Buenos Aires for ten days to see my girlfriend. My partner lived in a small studio and didn't have internet access—part of our daily ritual was going to a neighborhood cafe to log on. Mornings, she liked to sleep in. I'd get up a few hours before her, sit at the breakfast table, and write three or four sonnets, some in Donald Trump's voice, others addressed to him. I left Argentina with more than 30 new poems. Combined with the handful I'd written in November, I was halfway through a book.

I spent the next days in my Louisiana office space, holed up, continuing this chance Buenos Aires project, though the sonnet-writing wasn't as fluky as it sounds. More than twenty years earlier, I'd written a series of sonnets in the voice of comedians. Some time after that I'd written sonnets about writers, then sonnets about sports. And in 2006 I'd written a whole collection of sonnets about the 43rd president, George W. Bush. But even that latter project, which was completed over the course of three months, wasn't like this. By December 21, I had enough poems for a full-length volume. The next week, 50 days in, I pitched the project to Ridgeway Press, the Michigan publisher who'd done the Bush book, and received the go-ahead. A friend offered to format the manuscript during his time off around New Year's. The publisher and I both began looking for a printer. Everything fell into place and *Trump Sonnets, Volume 1* was in my hands by the inauguration.

For a month I happily sold books at various appearances. We did especially well at AWP, a big annual gathering of writers and writing teachers that was in Washington D.C. that year. Afterward, I finally had a short break, and the publisher and I sent books out for review. At a late February Mardi Gras party near Lafayette, Louisiana I brought a couple of dozen books, found a corner, and sold them 2-for-1 to friends there. Soon a number of strangers came by, one whispering conspiratorially, "You have something I know I want," before slipping me a twenty for two books, telling me to keep the change.

I left the party having sold all I brought.

About to leave for a mammoth four-month Western tour, I found myself once again writing a few Trump-inspired sonnets. Titling the first collection *Trump Sonnets, Volume 1* felt like a joke, but before I took off in early March, I challenged myself to finish a second collection before my early July return. Besides, many of the people I talked to wondered if I were working on a sequel, and, if so, whether I could keep up. Daily, there was something to respond to.

As I drove around the West this past spring, often working in very conservative places, I took my cues in how people responded to me.

In some conservative communities where I appeared primarily as a musician, I decided not to even display the new book with the rest of my merchandise, though was quick to mention it in one-to-one conversation if the talk veered that direction. At one public university, I was specifically asked not to mention the book at my event, which I thought was odd. At least there I made sure to display the book at the performance, where I sold a few copies.

But every place was different and it's all part of the narrative.

In Cochise County, southeast of Tucson, I spent three days in Sierra Vista, on staff for a writers' gathering. At the Thursday night opening, the four of us visiting writers each had five minutes to read work to introduce ourselves. I began by playing a fiddle tune and reciting a poem about old-time Appalachian fiddling, then read a short poem that partly explained the workshops I'd be leading the next two days. I closed by holding up *Trump Sonnets, Volume 1*, and reading "Trump Phoenix: Food," a poem in the president's voice. Later, a woman came up to buy the book, said she especially enjoyed the poem, and proudly identified herself as a Trump voter.

"You're not going to like the book," I told her.

"But I really liked that poem," she said.

"It's satire," I said. "Parody. You're not going to like the book."

"But I liked the poem. I'm a writer, too. I want to buy your book."

I could tell she was set to dig in. I shrugged my shoulders, took her twenty, made change.

A week and a half later in Dillon, Montana, I was walking downtown one afternoon after visiting the local elementary school as a guest of the local Arts Council. I passed a small independent bookstore, decided to turn around, stop in, and introduce myself. My idea was that since I had a children's book and two kids' CDs, maybe the proprietor would like to stock a few. But when I saw the display of work by Montana writer, Rick Bass, I took

Trump Sonnets from my backpack, and handed it to her. She flipped pages, then asked to see my other books. "I have more time tomorrow," she said. "Come back, and I'll buy five of that one from you, plus two of the children's book, and two of your memoir."

I smiled. "I know it's conservative here, similar to Alaska. Something like 60%. Right?"

The bookstore owner smiled back. "It's more like 80-20. Beaverhead County. But I already know at least five people who'll probably buy this. Bring the books tomorrow, write up an invoice; I'll give you a check."

In Spokane, my bookstore event in support of the new collection drew two dozen people on a cool Tuesday evening. The *Trump Sonnets* event had been listed in the store's monthly calendar along with a description of the new book. What I didn't know was that the preceding day the events manager, or one of the assistants, had sent an email promoting an evening of toe-tapping fiddle music plus Alaska-set poetry and storytelling with Alaska's Fiddling Poet—and didn't mention a word about the new Donald Trump-inspired book .

It had been almost a decade since I'd done any kind of bookstore tour, and these dates were fill-ins amid the paying gigs. It was new terrain for me, figuring how to publicly combine the fiddling and storytelling with the political poetry. The new material called for different pacing, different stories. So I started by playing mandolin, then fiddle, began talking, recited a music poem, then segued into the Trump material, telling stories of the past weeks in Sierra Vista and Dillon, reading a few poems from the book.

In the middle of the event, I asked if there were any questions. There were none, so I went on. At the end, I asked again if there any questions. A young man in the middle of the audience asked if I had poems that provided solutions, or at least better explained what people should be doing to confront Donald Trump.

"They're poems," I answered. "Sonnets. Hopefully, they're read, and enjoyed so people will want to reread them and think more critically about what's going on. I don't think there's one way through this, or that a book's function is to be didactic like that. But you might like this one."

Then I read the poem that was on one of the cards I'd placed on the seats, "To Donald Trump, from Berkeley" which included the lines: "The way/forward is to march, shout, write every day/and night. Donald, you're the double agent/of change, so change we must. We can't be silent/before you."

A woman then raised her hand, asked rhetorically why we couldn't at least give him a chance, and why was the country so divided. We needed a dialogue.

"Aren't we having a dialogue now?" I asked.

The woman beside her said, "Some of us here are part of the deplorables. We didn't enjoy this. We thought it was going to be something else. It was supposed to be fiddling."

It was only then at the tail end of the program that I learned that the bookstore had sent the email announcement, and hadn't mentioned the new book. I apologized for the misunderstanding, but explained why I'd come, and said that at least I'd played a few fiddle tunes, and shared a few poems set in Alaska.

The first woman who spoke then raised her hand. "He's not even taking a salary. Look at all he's doing for us. Why can't you give him a chance?"

In response, I read a last poem, one in the president's voice. Titled, "*Trump Newark: Language*" it was about emoluments, and how Trump explained that emoluments was a dumb word, part of a stupid story propagated by the failing *New York Times* because U.S. presidents had the right to do what they wanted. I'd given Donald Trump the last word, in a sense, but I couldn't help editorializing. Wasn't it obvious, I mused aloud, that he was profiting from the office in ways heretofore unseen?

That evening I sold several books and CDs, including three copies of the Trump book to a store employee who told me I should continue to do everything I could to get word out about the book.

The following week at a bookstore in Olympia, I asked the small audience, nearly all of whom had purchased the new book, what I could do to get more people at these events. One patron raised her hand, and announced I should go get myself arrested.

When I asked a similar question a day later in Seattle, about what I could do to get additional word out about this book in lieu of major national reviews, consensus was I ought to make YouTube videos of the poems, and see what happens. Maybe they'll go viral, one of the attendees said.

Recently I've uploaded eight videos to www.kenwaldman.com/trump-sonnets-volume-1 and www.kenwaldman.com/trump-sonnets-volume-2. Have they gone viral? Certainly not, and it's doubtful any of them will. But first, people have to know they exist, and I'm in process of making that happen.

A week after Seattle, at a show in Portland, Oregon, visibly enjoying myself as I randomly read one poem from the book after another, I mentioned that though most of what I'd been reading had been written five months earlier, they sounded like they could have been written yesterday. Or tomorrow. And that this writing was my process for dealing with the craziness. Reading them tonight in front of an appreciative audience felt healing, I continued.

"So we're all here as part of your therapy?" someone called from the back, and everybody
laughed.

Early August at a music festival in rural West Virginia, I carried copies of the book everywhere, along with my fiddle and mandolin. One afternoon, I even had an impromptu book release at my campsite, where I played tunes with friends, displayed the book on the hood of my car, and sold a few, offering the 2-for-1 discount I liked to give friends in informal settings. As I was packing up, a guitar player, who was camping two sites down, walked by, examined the book, shook his head, said he was one of the 70% of West Virginians who voted for Trump, then mentioned it was a shame how most all of his music buddies didn't see eye-to-eye with him.

I told him about the Arizona woman who was also a Trump supporter, who heard one of my poems and decided to buy the book,

"Read me that poem then," the guitarist said.

I read it, then looked at him to see what he thought.

"You seem like a nice enough fellow," the guitarist said, then went into his wallet, took out a twenty. "Keep the change," he said. "I'm a supporter of the arts."

"Two-for-one," I said, pocketing the cash, giving him a pair of books. "Maybe you'll want to pass one along to one of your pals."

He looked at me dubiously, but came up to me later in the week. "I did what you said, gave a copy to a friend. He was really appreciative. Thank you."

Trump Sonnets, Volume 3?

I haven't started it, have no idea what direction it might take if and when I do, but it wouldn't surprise me. For now, I've written 140 poems in 39 weeks, enough for two full-length poetry collections. Donald Trump is my muse, my bogeyman, my prompt to go talk about current events, no matter what.

As I wrote earlier here, every place is different and it's all part of the narrative.

It's a narrative that will continue, whether we participate, or not.

Crowdfunding For Poets (and Other Contrarians)

Confession #1: I still use a flip phone, which often makes people laugh when I take it out of my pocket.

Confession #2 (more to the point): at a February 2018 music conference, I attended a session about crowdfunding. The panelists agreed that for a successful crowdfunding campaign, a creator (those with projects are "creators") not only needed a huge swath of time to imagine, launch, and then oversee the campaign, but also needed a robust social media presence, and a familiarity with (if not love for) spreadsheets.

Confession #3 (even more germane): Despite having little free time, no social media presence, and no familiarity with, or interest in, spreadsheets, I launched a crowdfunding campaign in May 2018 to help my publisher, Ridgeway Press, bring out a book, *Trump Sonnets, Volume 3*. While the crowdfunding campaign ultimately proved successful, and some of the process played out as I hoped, some parts were truly a surprise.

When I say in the preceding paragraph that I had little free time, I'm not being entirely accurate. As a touring artist, I spend lots of time getting from place to place, and often it's in a car, driving, that I have time to think and to plan. That means time to consider budgets, and how to best make my way in the world in the coming weeks and months.

After having written *Trump Sonnets, Volume 1* (Ridgeway Press, 2017) and *Trump Sonnets, Volume 2* (Ridgeway Press, 2018), through fall and early winter 2018 I'd made headway on the next in the series. I'd composed the 2017 collection in a blur. Subtitled, *The First 50 Days*, I'd begun the manuscript the day after the 2016 U.S. presidential election, and by winter solstice had written 70 sonnets, more than half in Donald Trump's voice. Yes, it was satire, and calling it *Volume 1* was one of the jokes.

Before Christmas, I emailed the publisher, whom I had worked with a decade earlier, then phoned, and read him a few of the poems. Since it was so timely, he told me he wouldn't just accept the project, but that I could run with it. So I found a manufacturer that specialized in quick turn-arounds (and could design a functional cover with little fuss), had a friend willing to properly format the manuscript, and in that way had 400 copies in my hand by the inauguration. Small Press Distribution, where Ridgeway Press had an account, decided the book would officially have a March 2017 publication date. Because I had the copies in hand by the February 2017 AWP conference in Washington DC, we were able to quickly get the book into readers' and reviewers' hands.

It all felt like the right thing to do. We broke even almost immediately, so we ordered another run, this from a more economical manufacturer. Because the book had come out so soon, we'd missed every deadline for the more traditional reviews. But the response had been positive, which was heartening.

Though calling the first one *Volume 1* had been a joke, I soon found myself back on tour for four months, and writing more sonnets This president wasn't going to stop, so neither was I. By late June I'd written another 68 sonnets. The structure was near-identical to the prior book— half were commentaries; the rest were in Donald Trump's voice—but here the ones in Trump's voice were from what I imagined to be his dream life I phoned the publisher on Memorial Day from Southern California. Nearing completion of this second manuscript, I told him what I'd been doing. He offered to do this book too, which was to be titled, *Trump Sonnets, Volume 2*, its subtitle: *33 Commentaries, 33 Dreams*.

We had preview copies by mid-August, well in time for a January publication date. To put the project in context, I wrote an essay, "Donald Trump is My Muse," which I included in the review packets. Though the response was again strong from readers who found their way to the book, it failed to interest reviewers, or bookstores. Even the theater piece I was developing failed to attract attention.

    By January 2018, I was already well into writing *Volume 3*, where every sonnet was a reaction to the current United States president from the point of a view of a different nationality. Knowing I'd soon be finishing this book, driving several thousand miles from Louisiana to New England, then back, then Missouri, Georgia, Florida, North Carolina, and back to Louisiana, I thought about what next. If the reviewers weren't going to review the books, and if the vast majority of bookstores and libraries weren't going to order the books, and if the publisher and I weren't of means, what were we to do? The work not only felt worthy, but crucial. We were in an historic time.

    I may have been adverse to social media, me with my flip phone, but I wasn't adverse to writing the poems, and getting them to people who were enthusiastic about the project. While the conference session in Missouri made it clear that anyone who didn't use Facebook or Twitter didn't stand much of a chance with crowdfunding, the idea to crowdfund wouldn't leave me.

    Through February and March, I started reading more deeply about Kickstarter, Indiegogo, Gofundme, and learned of a British publisher, Unbound, which was using crowdfunding as its business model. When appropriate, I started asking friends and acquaintances about their experiences. Easter weekend I wrote a half-page newsletter, explaining the project I was considering. I described some of what I've been writing about here, and how Donald Trump was both everywhere and taboo, challenging and exhausting. Writing the first two books had been a fun and worthy antidote, I continued. But because book critics and booksellers, except for a few happy exceptions, had ignored the project, I decided that instead of going top down, the publisher and I would go bottom up. That was crowdfunding, and we'd have the readers fund the project from the start, and from there see what would happen.

I listed rewards: $25 would get a signed copy of the new book. $50, signed copies of all three books, plus a listing in the acknowledgment page. $100, we'd add three more books or CDs. $500, I'd come to do a solo show in the funder's community. $1,000, I'd come do a show with accompanists. Later, as we fleshed this out further, we added a $12 reward, where I'd mail eight poems from the collection to the supporter.

It took further thinking to decide how much to ultimately ask for in order to fully and successfully fund publication. From doing the past two *Trump Sonnets* books, I knew how much it would cost to print the books quickly, and how much to do a second, more economical run. Plus there would be the expenses of the crowdfunding campaign itself, from the making of a video—universally recommended—to mailing out the rewards (and taking into account foreign postage if it came to that).

I researched other campaigns on the various crowdfunding platforms, debated between asking for $4,000 and $5,000, and ultimately decided on $4,000. Within a week, I'd receive the omens that told me to definitely proceed.

Almost immediately after I composed the Easter weekend newsletter, I received an email from a musician friend I hadn't been in contact with since before the 2016 presidential election. He'd filled me in on what he'd been doing, then asked about me. I replied by including the just-written newsletter. The friend quickly wrote back and said once I officially launched the project, he'd be good for $100. It was just a few days later when another friend who I had reason to check in with, read the newsletter, and said that he'd like to contribute $500.

$600 was 15% of the final goal. Since I knew a lot more people I could reach out to directly in a way which felt comfortable to me, I felt confident I'd raise the money.

The next decision was which platform to ultimately choose.

For years I'd been receiving the email newsletter of a successful folk music artist who had what seemed a smart grasp on how to use social media and crowd-funding. My thinking in avoiding not only all social media but all email blasts was that while some people were more adept than others, on the whole we all already had too much electronic clutter in our lives—and I didn't want to add to it. So for years now I'd relied on postal mail, and found stationery which I liked, and stuffed each envelope with various cards and sheets that I thought would make sense to that particular recipient. After that initial correspondence, I'd follow up by one-to-one direct email, by site visit (or conference visit), and by phone. But that didn't mean I didn't pay attention to how others crafted their message to their own benefit.

For awhile I was leaning toward Indiegogo, primarily because this folk artist had used Indiegogo to successfully fund the latest CD project, but also because Indiegogo had an option that Kickstarter didn't. While Kickstarter, and most other platforms had an all-or-nothing model, meaning you either had to make your target total or receive nothing, Indiegogo allowed you to pocket whatever you raised, minus not just the usual percentage, but an additional fee. That sounded fine, since it took away the risk, and seemed to champion more transparency: whatever is donated will indeed be yours.

Then two things happened. First I made an appointment with a fiscal sponsor. I'd mistakenly thought whatever I raised through crowdfunding would first have to be funneled through a fiscal sponsor, a service I first obtained when I'd applied for a grant that needed to be under the auspices of a non-profit.

I spoke with my fiscal sponsor's representative who it turned out had both formerly backed numerous crowdfunding projects and had done a successful campaign herself. First, I learned I was wrong when I thought I needed a fiscal sponsor; anyone can register and try to earn money with a project. She strongly recommended Kickstarter, not just because it was older and more established, but because the all-or-nothing approach lent an urgency, which gave funders more incentive to invest. If I were to go on Kickstarter, she continued, she'd make a pledge since she thought the project worthy. On Indiegogo, she told me, she'd have to think about it, since it didn't feel like her support would be as necessary.

I was still leaning toward Indiegogo, when I had a chance phone discussion with a fellow musician, who had successfully used Indiegogo. She said that though she'd made her target and the money had been essential, some funders had complained that the platform continued to inundate them with emails for months. While the artist admitted that the funders could have changed their settings to quit receiving those emails, it had made for an unpleasant experience for some fans.

Before I committed to Kickstarter, I looked at GoFundMe, but quickly dismissed it since the emphasis was not on a creative project like this.

I also explored Unbound, the British publisher. The template, however, didn't allow me to proceed to the finish since I didn't have a regular social media presence. Though I researched the site, and reached out directly to two different Unbound staffers who I thought might be interested in this particular project, I never heard back from one. The other seemed to misunderstand the query.

In early May I paid a friend to help with a video. When I went live on May 14, he was the first to pledge. Soon, the one friend's $100 pledge officially was added to the total. By the end of the first week, the friend who said he'd contribute $500, made good. A day later I received another $500 pledge. By May 23 I had 14 backers, and had raised close to $1,500. I was 37% there.

While I might have put into practice what I heard at the music conference workshop session—the panelists all recommended no more than a 30-day pledge drive—I was simply too busy so decided on 50 days, ending on July 4 (another "mistake," according to the experts, ending on a holiday). My Louisiana rental had ended, so not only did I have to move, but I'd decided to put everything into storage. That necessitated going through boxes of books and papers, dumping what no longer served me. That took weeks. At some point around that time I bought a used car and sold my current car. I also had to drive to New England for work—the trip interrupted by a quick flight from Washington DC to Alaska in order to properly register the car at the DMV. The Kickstarter campaign couldn't always be the priority.

While I've always rebelled against writing in a journal, or doing a blog, or committing to any other regular writing task, for this project I did write an update every Tuesday, letting funders know the status of the project and what I'd been up to. Because of these updates, a few funders added to their original pledges.

While I'd have thought a project like this would have attracted interest from the huge community of Kickstarter backers, it wasn't like that. While I received a handful of pledges from strangers, including a surprise pledge from Singapore, what support I received mostly came from friends I'd contacted directly. For some, this was their first time ever pledging on any crowdfunding platform.

I'd been warned there might be a lull in raising money, and that was true here. Having reached 37% in the first ten days, it wasn't until June 20, two weeks before the deadline, that I reached $3,000, or 75% of my goal. By then I had 45 backers. One constant was my Tuesday updates. Another, the surprise upon learning which of my contacts contributed, and their level of generosity and support.

Here I was, a freelance writer, musician, and educator, who made a living as a touring artist. There were many ways to go about earning money and I'd never have considered myself particularly adept at fundraising. I relied mainly on appearances, though that didn't always get me everywhere I felt I had to go. On Kickstarter I could make my case for a third round of *Trump Sonnets*. On June 23, a pledge of $275 lifted me just above $3,400. I was 85% there with more than ten days to go.

I was going to spend July 4 with friends in Austin, one of them the designer of the two previous books in the series. I drove through the night of July 1 from Louisiana, spent the morning of July 2 in a coffeehouse, sending emails to friends. The past week had been another lull and I still hadn't topped $4,000. But I was getting closer. I had 57 backers and needed another $150. We had three days left, and I didn't want to leave anything to chance. If we were short, I'd receive nothing.

One friend wrote to say she was monitoring the pledges and if I needed her support, she'd contribute. Two others, both of whom who had previously pledged $100, wrote to say they would contribute more if it came to that. It was helpful to know I had them as back-ups, but I didn't want to have to go back to them. The morning of July 2, I wrote to several friends who I thought would be receptive, but hadn't responded to my earlier requests.

By that afternoon, I'd received four more pledges, and had topped $4,000. I celebrated with friends over a beer. The next two days, another $200 came in, enough to not only allow the publisher and I to bring out *Trump Sonnets, Volume 3*, but also to launch trumpsonnets.com for a year; the domain name was available.

Within a month, we manufactured books for its 2019 release.

Once again our media contacts have declined to review the project, or the accompanying theater piece, now called, in a nod to Dr. Strangelove, *Trump Sonnets or: How I've Taken on Donald Trump (and Won)*. The publisher and I are still hand-selling the books. I marvel how I've never had a project easier to sell to some people. 99.99% of those who loathe the current president may be exhausted by the drama, but that other .01% wonder why they haven't heard of these books, and are excited to buy one or more. That .01% is still a lot of people.

I'm not sure how else this third book in the series would have been published in a timely way without crowdfunding. Raising money in that way removed our risk. It's why Unbound in England, and its staff of book industry veterans, has chosen this as its commercial publishing model.

One of my friends who pledged support, later bought four sets of books for holiday presents, and then reported a hard-to-please sister was particularly delighted. She added if I came back to her with another project, she'd be sure to support that too.

Maybe I'd have raised an additional several thousand dollars if I'd followed the advice I'd heard from the crowdfunding experts. But I did this work in a way that made sense to me.

I believe all writers, no matter their experience in crowdfunding and social media, can do this if they have a project they deeply believe in, and have written it well. When I have another manuscript that fits the definition, I'll try it again myself. Writers and publishers need all the help they can muster.

26
Today's Manifesto

Have pen and paper handy (never leave home without at least three pens and one small notebook).

Read your contemporaries, read the classics, reread favorites, read interviews, read discussions of craft (never leave home without a book).

Pay attention (a moment can change—or save—a life; a moment can change—or save—the world).

Cultivate dreams (both day and night).

Acknowledge birthdays, holidays, marriages, deaths; acknowledge this minute (as you sit at a desk or curl in a chair, remember that any occasion, big or small, may be transcendent—or at least authentic).

When in doubt, write a sonnet (or villanelle, sestina, pantoum).

When in despair, imagine what you've never imagined (and swore you never would).

When happy, celebrate quietly (be steady, my friend).

When stuck, take a nap, or go for a walk (and when shutting the door behind you, yes, have pens and notebook).

Honor your best teachers (and aim to surpass them).

Support public libraries and local bookstores (and like-minded writers and publishers).

Read your work aloud (then read it aloud again).

Don't try to please everybody (just yourself, and perhaps one or two others).

Be generous; offer help (and not only to friends).

Be clear-eyed and strong (not obscure and glib); write tough poems (not nice ones).

Be playful (arranging words on a page can make for serious fun); start new poems using prompts you otherwise wouldn't contemplate (pretend you're someone else).

Bust taboos (when need arises); be greedy (with time); steal (if appropriate).

Steal? (Recall the lines: "when a nurse asked/my religion, I answered/'poetry.'" Writing poetry may not be your religion, but it's a way to navigate the world: so steal an idea, scavenge a line, do what you must.)

Trust yourself (you always know best).

Explore obsessions (go deeper).

Stop talking about writing you're not doing (write badly as opposed to not writing at all).

Be wary of rhyme and metaphor, and of any word or phrase that draws attention to itself and away from the poem (figurative language is a tool, not an end).

Swear off safety and predictability (and, of course, cliché).

Have a dictionary and thesaurus nearby (whether on a shelf or website—and while a computer with internet access may feel absolutely essential, you can write books without one).

Seek feedback (one on-target response can rescue virtually anything).

Dismiss skeptics (and call out the bullies among them).

Reject rejection (though be open to multiple revision).

Cut words, phrases, lines, stanzas (make a ruthless game of it).

Surprise yourself (take delight in chance accidents that invariably will also surprise readers).

Count syllables (ruminate over line breaks).

Do what you love (even on days you don't much want to).

Welcome in good luck (and accept the bad without excessive complaint).

Identify serendipity, synchronicity, signs (and recognize when to pack it in and go to bed).

Remember that yours is the long, slow way (even when in a rush or on deadline, even amidst success).

Allow time to complete a reasonable working draft (then let the piece be before going back to shape it further).

Have a few minutes? Start a new poem (start *two* new poems).

Save old notebooks and the odd scraps of paper (and hope when you return you can decipher the scrawl).

Be contrary if you must (but gracefully, with a sense of humor).

Resist self-sabotage (at least your usual kind).

Honor voices (the strange, the simple, the sublime).

Sing (as no one has ever sung) and tell stories (that no one has ever told).

Repetition is fine (and is to be commended—but, please, don't keep repeating yourself).

Make lists (presumably with one of your pens).

Accept the mess and the contradictions (or suffer accordingly).

Deviate when necessary from any of the above (don't stick to any one process, save the process of living).

Persist (survive).

Don't forget (no, never forget) that these principles will change (yes, they will change tomorrow).

27
Endings

How to end a poem, story, essay, or book?

Like every answer, it depends on the circumstance. Here's a general tip: it never hurts to somehow refer back to the beginning, adding a little bit extra, what folks in Louisiana call *lagniappe*. It never hurts to revise until you get it right, then revise some more. An excellent beginning lures a reader in. An excellent middle keeps a reader engaged. An excellent ending leaves a reader satisfied.

In this case, I've returned to both the first chapter and the introduction, which preceded it. If I'd have ended with a block of poetry — a party of sonnets or not — no matter how effectively those poems amplified the rest of the writing, this would have felt somehow incomplete. How did I know? I had no outline. But when I got to that last poem, the manuscript felt unfinished, and I understood there needed to be this one last section after also adding recent essays to bring the book up-to-date.

One more truism: a piece of writing is *never* fully complete, is *always* abandoned at some point, and can *always* be improved. As someone who's worn glasses since age seven, I've come to think of it like this: every time I revise in any way, whether adding, subtracting, or moving single words, whole phrases, sentences, paragraphs, or chapters, I consider that revision as if trying different prescription lenses at the optometrist's.

Do I now see better or worse?

In other words, have I sharpened the work or made it blurrier?

Occasionally I'll finish a piece quickly and be done with it. Usually I'll see more over time, and revise accordingly. But at some point, the changes become so subtle that I can't even tell if it's better. And when I can't tell if I'm improving a piece of writing that I'm working on, then it's time to move on, at least until I get a nagging feeling there's something still undone, and then I go take it out, and give it another a look.

I'll often tell classes that when we start a new piece we're all equal before a blank piece of paper. The only reason that I'm teaching, and I've been published, is that once I get something down, I'll keep at it doggedly, then keep at it some more.

I'll begin a workshop with an icebreaker.

I'll end with a reminder of what all we've done the past hours, or weeks. If we haven't already, I'll remind attendees to exchange business cards—I've already given out mine!—or share other contact information, as appropriate. We've come together as a group, done some writing, and had our fun. Then comes the leaving. Lots of people think what comes next is the hard part, continuing the work in solitude. It *is* hard, yet it's not. It's only writing, and that part is fun too.

But we haven't left yet. I promise that if anyone contacts me, I'll get back in touch. I thank them for coming. In our increasingly busy lives, it's no small thing to spend time (and, often, money) in a room with other writers. It's also no small thing to spend time (and, often, money) reading a book like this.

I've just been rereading Richard Hugo's *Triggering Town*. I don't mark up my books, but if I did I'd underline this sentence near the end of the sixth chapter: "A creative-writing class may be one of the last places you can go where your life still matters."

Writing poetry, fiction, nonfiction, plays, screenplays isn't for everyone. Again, you can get what you need from parenting, gardening, cooking, mountain climbing, attending church, shooting photos. But writing is special in that it can encompass every one of those activities, and more. Done well, I believe it can help change your life, or at least point you how to better manage the one you have now.

In the introduction, I shared two poems, one about a party in Nome, the other a sonnet for a favorite writer William Stafford. I ended one of the preceding chapters with a sonnet I wrote for what would have been Stafford's one hundredth birthday. Here, I'll share the other two poems I've written for William Stafford. The first, I wrote while visiting Fairbanks in 1993 a few months after Stafford passed away. The second, a villanelle which has appeared in an anthology of Stafford-inspired poetry, I wrote several years later.

William Stafford atop Mt. Ripinski

Forty-two hundred feet closer
to an August sky the clear blue
of eyes, having climbed a last breezy
bare-rock mound beyond meadow and brush,
he faced up to heaven and saw
past his desire to love and be loved,

until he sat to take in that rare
long view of southeast Alaska water
and wood. Rapt, he dug in his pack
for an apple, cheese, a book
which he read from. Then he slept,
his head on worn paper cover,
through which spoke the poems.

Villanelle for William Stafford

It should be something easy,
should that word to watch for.
A word that's easy

to use *and* misuse. You'll agree,
or disagree, that *should* is like *more*—
it *should* be something easy,

but maybe not. More or less, we
live our lives before
words that are easy

to mistake: work, family, country,
love. We come and go. It's either or.
It should be something easy,

shouldn't it, *it* being the tree
to climb, the brush to clear, the four
words that are easy

to line and break: *How to free
ourselves?* To open that door—
it should be something easy—
one word. And then the next. Easy.

MEZCALITA PRESS

An independent publishing company dedicated to bringing the printed poetry, fiction, and non-fiction of musicians who want to add to the power and reach of their important voices.

Other works by Ken Waldman

Poetry and Prose:
Sports Page (Lamar University Literary Press, 2020)
Trump Sonnets, Volume 4 (Ridgeway Press, 2020)
Trump Sonnets, Volume 3 (Ridgeway Press, 2019)
Trump Sonnets, Volume 2 (Ridgeway Press, 2018)
Trump Sonnets, Volume 1 (Ridgeway Press, 2017)
D is for Dog Team (Nomadic Press children's book, 2009)
Are You Famous? (Catalyst Book Press, 2008)
As the World Burns (Ridgeway Press, 2006)
Conditions and Cures (Steel Toe Books, 2006)
And Shadow Remained (Pavement Saw Press, 2006)
The Secret Visitor's Guide (Wings Press, 2006)
To Live on This Earth (West End Press, 2002)
Nome Poems (West End Press, 2000)

Recordings:
D is for Dog Team (Nomadic Press, 2009)
Some Favorites (Nomadic Press, 2009)
55 Tunes, 5 Poems (Nomadic Press, 2008)
As the World Burns (Nomadic Press, 2006)
All Originals, All Traditionals (Nomadic Press, 2006)
Fiddling Poets on Parade (Nomadic Press, 2006)
Music Party (Nomadic Press, 2003)
Burnt Down House (Nomadic Press, 2001)
A Week in Eek (Nomadic Press, 2000)

www.ingramcontent.com/pod-product-compliance
Lightning Source LLC
Chambersburg PA
CBHW031136160426
43193CB00008B/153